# knit hats!

## 15 Cool Patterns to Keep You Warm

Edited by GWEN STEEGE

STOREY
BOOKS

The mission of Storey Publishing is to serve our customers by publishing practical information that encourages personal independence in harmony with the environment.

**Edited by** Gwen Steege, Susan Huxley, and Karen Levy
**Designed by** Susi Oberhelman
**Cover photograph** by Giles Prett
**Photographs by** Robin Holland
**Headforms by** Carleton Woodworking, 195 Adams Street, 8G, Brooklyn, NY 11201, 718.417-1600, carleton @ CWWing.com
**Illustrations by** Alison Kolesar
**Text production by** Jennifer Jepson Smith and Jen Rork
**Indexed by** Susan Olason

Printed in China by C&C Offset Printing Co., Ltd.
10 9 8 7 6 5 4 3 2 1

**Library of Congress Cataloging-in-Publication Data**
Knit hats! : 15 cool patterns to keep you warm / Edited by Gwen Steege.
p. cm.
ISBN 1-58017-482-5
1. Knitting—Patterns. 2. Hats. I. Steege, Gwen, 1940-
TT825 .K628 2002
746.43'20432--dc21
2002007750

# Contents

Hats Off to Knitting!                4

Carrot Top                          18

Watch Cap                           22

Three-in-One                        26

Slip-a-Color                        32

Color Me Bright                     36

Three-Gauge Beret                   40

Pillbox Flowers                     44

Bunnies and Carrots                 48

Morning Glories                     56

Handpaint Hat                       62

Double-Knit Headband                66

Needle-Felted Hat                   72

Felted Sherpa Hat                   76

Adult's Felt Hat                    82

Child's Felt Hat                    86

Index                               94

# Hats Off to Knitting!

Few knitting projects are more satisfying than hats. Most are quick and easy to knit and, because they take a small amount of yarn, they are relatively inexpensive as well. Usually knitted all in one piece ("in the round"), a hat is really a three-dimensional sculpture — you can see the hat taking shape as you knit. And whether you wear your hat or give it away, your unique creation is right out there for all to admire.

For this collection of patterns from seven North American designers, we've chosen a variety of styles for sizes ranging from baby to adults. Some are just plain fun, others are glamorous — all are practical and warm. If you're only beginning to knit and want something easy, or if you're more experienced but need a project you can do in a hurry, notice the patterns marked "Easy!" If you're looking for more of a challenge, the headbands on page 66 are the ideal introduction to double-knitting. And if you haven't experimented with felted knitting, take a look at the "sherpa" helmets for babies or the shaped hats for little girls or women on pages 76, 82, and 86.

## A Good Yarn

One of the best things about knitting these days is the wonderful variety of colors, textures, and weights of yarns that easily lure you into yarn shops. When you're deciding what kind of yarn to choose — wool, mohair, cashmere, angora, alpaca, silk, rayon, cotton, linen, synthetic, and various blends — consider how the hat will be used and what the wearer prefers. Will this hat be worn for fun, or does it need to be thick and warm and fit over the ears? Many knitters prefer natural fibers for their hand knits. Wool, for instance, is considered warmer than acrylic, even when wet, but some folks find wool itchy, or they may even be allergic to it. If you're knitting a baby hat, a good compromise is washable wool, which is soft and easy to care for.

For two-color knitting, choose yarns of the same fibers and weight. Different yarn fibers have different degrees of elasticity, or they may differ in the way they knit up, hold their shape, and wash.

In terms of yarn quality, as with most products, you are likely to get what you pay for. Very inexpensive yarns stretch easily and pill and, in general, don't hold up well. Knitting is a fun hobby, but when you're putting time and effort into a project, you'll want it to last. Following

## Avoiding the Itch Factor

If you dislike having wool against your skin, choose a hat style with a wide hem, and knit this hem of a fiber other than wool — cotton or silk, for instance.

are some general yarn categories and their average gauges and needle sizes.

**Baby or fingering yarn**
6.5 to 8 stitches = 1 inch     US 0-3

**Sport weight yarn**
5.5 to 6 stitches = 1 inch     US 4-6

**DK (double knit) yarn**
5 to 6 stitches = 1 inch     US 4-6

**Worsted weight yarn**
4 to 5 stitches = 1 inch     US 6-9

**Bulky weight yarn**
2 to 3.5 stitches = 1 inch     US 9-11

**Chunky weight yarn**
3.5 to 4 stitches = 1 inch     US 9–10½

If you're substituting a yarn for the one recommended in a pattern, make sure you purchase the correct amount of yardage. For instance, if a pattern calls for one skein of a certain yarn that is packaged 190 yards to a skein and you want to substitute it with a yarn packaged in 100-yard skeins, you'll need to buy two skeins of the substitute yarn. You can usually find this information right on the label, or ask the yarn shop. You'll find yarns come in circular skeins that must be wound into balls before use, as well as in pull-out skeins that don't need rewinding; for a smoother feed, take the yarn from the inside of these skeins.

It's always best to buy an extra skein or two to avoid running short. If you have to return for more yarn, you may find that the yarn shop is either out of it or that what they have is from a different dye lot, which means the colors may be slightly but noticeably different. Some yarn shops will set aside an additional skein for up to a month, just in case you need another; most shops will also accept unused skeins for cash or credit.

## Need Some Needles?

Most knitters have strong preferences when it comes to selecting knitting needles, and the wide variety of choices can be confusing until you try them. Coated aluminum needles are durable but sometimes heavy in larger sizes. Plastic or similar materials are lighter, though they can bend or break. Bamboo needles have become increasingly popular: yarn moves smoothly along bamboo needles, even in hot, sticky weather, and they're comfortable and quiet to use.

Available in several lengths, straight needles are easy to work with. Some people find shorter needles easier to manage. For projects that don't fit easily onto short, straight needles, use circular needles. You'll also need circular or double-pointed needles to knit cylindrical shapes, such as mittens and hats. Most of the hats in this book are knit in the round on circular or double-pointed needles. Circular needles come in different lengths and have a flexible nylon or plastic center. The 16-inch length is usually most appropriate for adult-size hats.

## Stocking Up

Depending on the project you are knitting, you don't need to purchase all of these items at once. But a well-supplied knitting bag, like all toolkits, makes life easier in many ways.

- Sets of needles, including straight, double-pointed, and circular
- Set of crochet hooks
- A 6-inch metal ruler with a needle gauge
- Retractable tape measure
- Needle point covers
- Assortment of blunt-pointed tapestry needles
- Box of T-shaped pins
- Small, sharp scissors
- Stitch holders
- Stitch markers, both round and split
- Nice knitting bag

Double-pointed needles are used for knitting in the round. You may need to switch from circular to double-pointed needles when you're decreasing a hat to make the top of the crown, and the stitches on the circular needle stretch too far apart to work. When possible, choose a set of double-pointed needles that comes five to a package. Some patterns require five needles, but even if not, it's always good to have the extra needle in case you lose one.

You also need a set of crochet hooks for picking up dropped stitches, weaving in ends, and finishing some edges.

Needles come in numbered sizes, but it's important to note whether the size is US, UK, or metric — they're all different! You'll quickly notice that in the US system, 0 is very small; in the UK system, 0 is large. This book provides US and metric sizes in all the instructions. To convert to other systems, follow the chart:

| US | Metric | UK |
|----|--------|-----|
| 0 | 2mm | 14 |
| 1 | 2¼mm | 13 |
| | 2½mm | |
| 2 | 2¾mm | 12 |
| | 3mm | 11 |
| 3 | 3¼mm | 10 |
| 4 | 3½mm | |
| 5 | 3¾mm | 9 |
| 6 | 4mm | 8 |
| 7 | 4½mm | 7 |
| 8 | 5mm | 6 |
| 9 | 5½mm | 5 |
| 10 | 6mm | 4 |
| 10½ | 6½mm | 3 |
| | 7mm | 2 |
| | 7½mm | 1 |
| 11 | 8mm | 0 |
| 13 | 9mm | 00 |
| 15 | 10mm | 000 |

## Getting Gauge Right

It may seem like a nuisance, but, in the long run, knitting an accurate stitch gauge with the yarn and needles you'll be using for your project is one of the most important knitting techniques — no matter how experienced you are as a knitter. The stitch gauge (sometimes called tension) is the number of stitches per inch that you need to make to produce the right size. Obtaining the right gauge can make the difference between a hat that fits properly and one that is unwearable.

Always calculate your gauge over 4 inches (10cm). That's because counting stitches over 1 inch (2.5cm) can be misleading if your stitches are uneven or if the recommended stitches per inch contains a fraction. Here's an example of how to knit a swatch and figure out gauge:

1. Say a pattern lists the gauge as 16 stitches = 4 inches on size 7 needles. Use size 7 needles to cast on 20 stitches (this is the number of gauge stitches, plus a few extra so that you don't need to measure the edge stitches, which may be uneven).
2. Following the stitch pattern you'll be using for the main part of your project (unless the pattern indicates otherwise), knit a swatch about 4 inches long. Do not block the swatch.
3. Lay the swatch on a firm, flat surface. Take care not to stretch the swatch, and make sure the side

edges are uncurled. Lay a flat ruler from one side of the swatch to the other. Count the number of stitches within 4 inches (10cm). There should be exactly 16.

4. *If your swatch contains more than 16 stitches in 4 inches,* use larger needles and knit another swatch. Repeat steps 1 through 3.
5. *If your swatch contains fewer than 16 stitches in 4 inches,* use smaller needles and knit another swatch. Repeat steps 1 through 3.

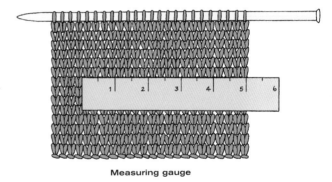

**Measuring gauge**

**NOTE:** Always use fresh yarn to make a swatch. Used yarn may be stretched and thus give an inaccurate measurement.

Also, two needle sizes are sometimes specified for a pattern, the larger for the main body of the hat, and the smaller for ribbing, for instance. If you change your larger-size needle to obtain the correct stitch gauge, adjust the size of the smaller needle to correspond.

## Knitting-ese

To make instructions more concise, most knitters use abbreviations. If you're new to knitting, they can seem like a foreign language. You may encounter these:

| | |
|---|---|
| **cc** | contrasting color |
| **cm** | centimeter |
| **cont** | continue |
| **dec** | decrease/decreasing |
| **dp** | double pointed |
| **g** | gram |
| **inc** | increase/increasing |
| **K** | knit |
| **K2tog** | knit 2 stitches together |
| **M1** | make 1 |
| **mc** | main color |
| **mm** | millimeter |
| **P** | purl |
| **P2tog** | purl 2 stitches together |
| **psso** | pass slip stitch over |
| **pu** | pick up |
| **rep** | repeat |
| **rem** | remaining |
| **rnd(s)** | round(s) |
| **sl** | slip |
| **sl st** | slip stitch |
| **ssk** | slip, slip, knit 2 together |
| **st(s)** | stitch(es) |
| **St st** | stockinette stitch |
| **yd(s)** | yard(s) |
| **YO** | yarn over |

## It's Only Fitting

Most of the hats in this book can be knitted in several sizes. To obtain the best fit, measure the circumference of the wearer's head before you knit, and use the instructions for the size closest to that measurement. No one wants a hat to slip around, so the hat circumference may be smaller than the head it's designed to fit. The difference between head and hat size can vary, depending on the hat's "cuff" (for example, rolled stockinette stitch or ribbing) and the type of yarn (stretchy or firm).

To measure head size, begin at the top middle of the forehead just below the hairline. Run a tape measure in front of the ears, around the back of the neck, and back up to the forehead. Compare that to the average head sizes listed below. Unless otherwise noted in the pattern, refer to these measurements when you decide which size to knit.

| | |
|---|---|
| **Baby** | 14½–16 inches (37–41cm) |
| **Child** | 17–18½ inches (43–47cm) |
| **Adult S** | 19–20 inches (48.5–51cm) |
| **Adult M** | 21 inches (52.5cm) |
| **Adult L** | 22–24 inches (56–61cm) |

## Casting Call

**Casting on** with a **long-tail cast on** makes an especially neat, firm, but elastic edge for a hat cuff. If you tend to cast on tightly, you may want to switch to one needle size larger for this part.

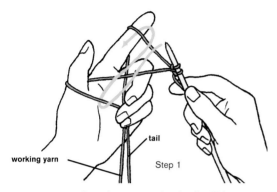

working yarn

tail

Step 1

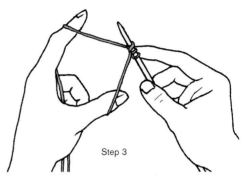

Step 3

1. Estimate how long to make the "tail" by wrapping the yarn around the needle one time for each cast-on stitch you need, then adding a few extra inches. Make a slip knot right here, and slide the knot over a single knitting needle. Hold that needle in your right hand; hold the tail and the working end of the yarn in your left hand. Insert needle through front loop of working yarn loop on your thumb. Wrap tail from back to front around needle.

3. Release loop on your thumb, place your thumb underneath the working thread, and draw both toward you while holding the working thread and tail firmly in your fingers.

**Casting off** is sometimes called binding off. If you tend to cast off tightly, you may want to switch to one needle size larger. The simplest way to cast off is to knit two stitches to the right-hand needle, then draw the first one over the second. Don't pull too tightly, or your edge will be puckered and inelastic. When you reach the last stitch, pull the working end through the stitch and weave it into the inside.

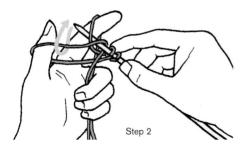

Step 2

2. Use needle to draw tail through the loop on your thumb.

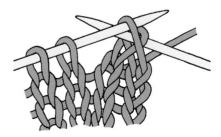

# On the Increase

Increases allow you to shape your knitting as you work. Sometimes you'll want these increases to be invisible, but in other cases the increase stitches are not only noticeable but important design elements. It's helpful to learn a variety of techniques so that you can pick and choose whatever is appropriate for your needs. The illustrations that follow show three increase methods: bar increase, make 1 with a right slant, and make 1 with a left slant.

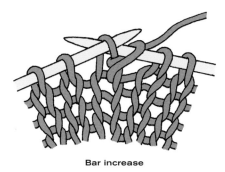

**Bar increase**

The bar increase is a tight increase that leaves no hole, but shows as a short, horizontal bar on the right side of the fabric. Make it by knitting into the front of the loop in the usual way, but do not remove the stitch from the needle. Instead, knit into the back of the same stitch, and slip both new stitches onto the right needle.

**To increase by two stitches,** work into the front loop, the back loop, and the front loop again before taking the three new stitches off the needle.

## Make 1, right slant

**1.** Look for the horizontal bar between the first stitch on your left-hand needle and the last stitch on your right-hand needle. With the tip of your left needle, pick up this bar from back to front.

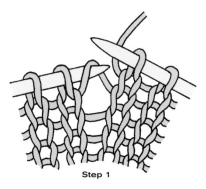

**Step 1**

**2.** Knit into the bar from the front, which twists the new stitch and gives it a slant to the right. Even though it may seem a bit difficult to get your needle into the bar from front to back, it's important to do so in order to avoid creating a small hole in the fabric.

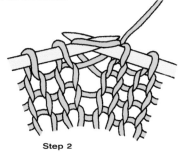

**Step 2**

### Make 1, left slant

**1.** Pick up the bar from front to back.

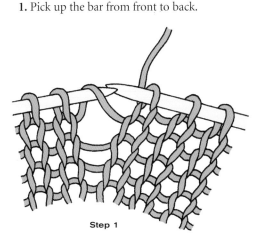

Step 1

**2.** Knit into the back of the bar, which twists the new stitch to the left.

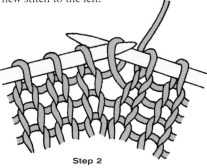

Step 2

**NOTE:** To make 1 at the end of a round, pick up the horizontal strand between the first and the last stitch of the round.

## No-Stress Pickup

Beginning knitters often panic when they drop a stitch. It's empowering to discover how easy it is to pick up dropped or half-made stitches. And this is why you need to include a crochet hook in your knitting bag!

Working on the right side of stockinette stitch, find the last loop that's still knitted and insert the crochet hook from front to back. Pull the loop just above the bar between the adjacent stitches, catch the bar with your hook, and draw it through the loop. The result should look exactly like a knitted stitch. If you have to pick up a number of stitches, take care to pick up the bars in the correct order.

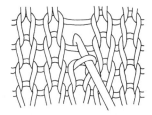

Picking up a dropped stitch knitwise

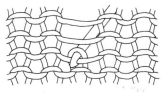

Picking up a dropped stitch purlwise

# On the Decrease

As with increasing, decreasing can become an interesting design element in your project, and the pattern directions will specify which method to use. There are three common techniques. Because the first two result in a finished stitch that slants to the left, it is often used at the right side of a garment; the last method results in a right-slanting stitch and so is used on the left edge.

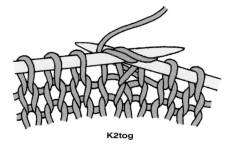

**K2tog**

**K2tog.** The second technique is simply to knit two stitches together by inserting the needle into both loops, just as you would to knit. The finished stitch slants to the right on the finished side and is generally used at the end of a row.

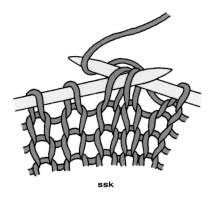

**ssk**

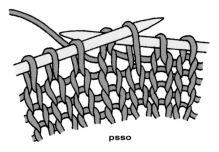

**psso**

**ssk.** The first method is called "ssk" (slip, slip, knit two stitches together). Slip two stitches, *one at a time,* from your left needle to your right, as if to knit. Then, slide the left needle from left to right through the front loops of the slipped stitches, and knit the two stitches together from this position. This technique makes a finished stitch that slants to the left on the finished side and is often used at the beginning of a row.

**psso.** The third decrease is often referred to as "psso" (pass slip stitch over knit stitch). In a knit row, slip one stitch from the left needle to the right needle, inserting the needle as if to knit the stitch, but without knitting it. Knit the next stitch, then use the left needle to draw the slipped stitch over the just-knitted stitch. This technique makes a finished stitch that slants to the left on the finished side and is often used at the beginning of a row.

## Joining New Yarn

When you run out of yarn and need to start a new end, it's best to do so toward the edge of the garment, where the join is less likely to be noticed. Perhaps the easiest and strongest method is to lay the new yarn over the old yarn so that you can knit the two together for three or four stitches, then drop the old yarn and continue with the new. When you come to those doubled stitches in the next row, be sure to knit the two yarns together as one. Be aware that if the yarn you're using is very smooth, plain, and/or inelastic, this kind of join may show.

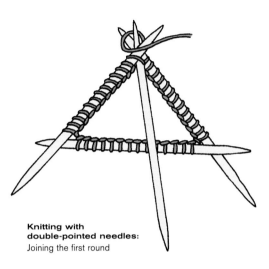

**Knitting with double-pointed needles:**
Joining the first round

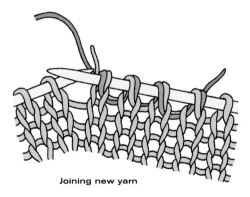

**Joining new yarn**

## Knitting in the Round

When you knit in the round to make stockinette stitch, you always knit on the right side, continuing around the circular or double-pointed needles without ever turning your work. (On straight needles, stockinette is created by knitting on one side, turning, and purling on the return). For small projects like mittens or baby hats, use double-pointed needles to knit in the round; for larger tubes, use circular needles.

**To knit with double-pointed needles,** cast on the correct number of stitches for your project, and divide the stitches evenly among three of the needles (or as the pattern directs). Lay the work on a flat surface, forming the three needles into a triangle. Arrange the cast-on stitches so they are flat and all facing toward the center of the triangle. Look carefully along the needles and especially at the corners to make sure that the stitches don't take an extra twist around the needle.

The next step is the trickiest: Carefully lift the needles, keeping the stitches aligned, and use the working yarn that formed the last cast-on stitch to knit the first stitch on the left-hand needle. Snug the

## Tips for Knitting with Double-Pointed Needles

- To avoid the common problem of loose stitches that develop where the needles change, make sure that each time you reach those corners you snug the yarn firmly after knitting the first stitch on the new needle.
- After the first round is complete, check again to be sure no stitches have twisted around the needles. You want your finished project to be a nice tubular mitten, not a Mobius strip!
- To make knitting easier, arrange your needles so the ends of the two you are working with lay on top of the third needle.

yarn firmly before knitting the second stitch. (Do not tie to join.) Knit across until the left-hand needle is empty. Use the empty needle to knit the stitches on the next needle. Continue knitting until the first round is complete. Place a marker on the needle to indicate the beginning of each new round.

**To knit with circular needles,** cast on the correct number of stitches as usual, then lay the work on a flat surface. Arrange the stitches facing the center of the circle and carefully knit the first couple of stitches on the left-hand needle, taking care not to twist any stitches around the needles. Snug the yarn tightly between the last cast-on stitch and the first stitch in the first round. (Do not tie to join.) Place a marker between these two stitches to help you keep track of rounds.

**Knitting stripes in the round** creates a little jog where you end one color and start the next. Here's an easy way to fix this problem:

1. When you change yarn color at the end of one stripe and beginning of the next, cut the yarn, leaving a tail about 6 inches long. Don't carry along the unused color.

2. When the knitting is finished, turn the project inside out so the wrong side (inside) is facing you. Thread the yarn that started the stripe onto a tapestry needle and pull it diagonally through the back of the stitches at the jog — up and to the left.

3. Sew the remaining yarn tail at the top of the stripe diagonally down and to the right, through the back of the stitches. Weave in the ends for several stitches.

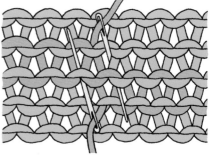

**Disguising jog in stripes**

## Colorful Effects

An infinite number of fascinating designs can be created by knitting with two or more colors in a single row or round. In this book, we illustrate the sequence of multicolor knitting in charts that are color-matched to the photos of the finished projects. When you follow a chart, be sure to start at the bottom right corner, working from right to left and bottom to top. (This makes perfect sense when you realize this is exactly the way your knitted hat is evolving as well.)

When you knit more than three stitches in one color, then switch back to a previous color, carry the previous color along on the wrong side, keeping the carried yarn loose so that it doesn't pucker. Don't carry the yarn for more than three stitches or you'll end up with long loops that can get snagged by the wearer. To avoid this, catch the carried yarn under the working yarn every three or four stitches, as shown.

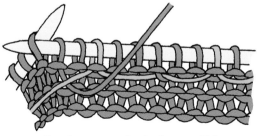

**Carrying a second color (wrong side)**

## Do Be a Blockhead

You may be anxious to wear your beautiful new hat, but do take the time to weave all loose ends in on the wrong side of the fabric, then block it properly. You'll be surprised at how any unevenness disappears when you block your knitting.

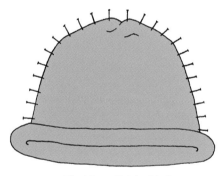

**Blocking a finished hat**

You can steam-block all-wool fabrics by holding a steam iron just above the surface so the steam penetrates the fabric, or cover the surface with a wet pressing cloth and lightly touch the iron to it. Either way, avoid pressing hard or moving the iron back and forth.

For wool blends, mohair, angora, alpaca, or cashmere, just dampen the knitted piece by spraying it lightly with water, then pin it to a flat surface where you can safely leave it to air-dry. Be sure to pin it so the dimensions are correct and the stitches are lined up straight.

## The Seamy Side

With a few exceptions, a simple running stitch is best for sewing together seams on hats, because it has the elasticity to match the hat's potential stretch.

1. Place the pieces to be seamed with the right sides together and pin them in place, with the edges neatly aligned.
2. Thread a blunt tapestry needle with the same yarn with which you knit the hat. Starting at the bottom edge, insert the needle from the top, leaving a 4-inch tail of yarn (you'll weave this in later).
3. Make small stitches just inside the first stitches along the outer edge of the hat. Continue to the end. Weave both tails of yarn through several knit stitches in the seam allowance. Cut the yarn.

Sewing a seam with the running stitch

## Finishes and Flourishes

Of course you can always finish a hat with a plain crown, but when you want to add a flourish to the top of a hat, here are several favorites: I-cords, pompoms, and tassels.

### I-CORDS

I-cords are narrow cylinders knitted on two double-pointed needles. The project directions will specify the number of stitches — usually 3 or 4.

1. Using double-pointed needles, cast on 3 (or 4) stitches; knit 3 (or 4).
2. Slide the stitches to the other end of the needle so the first cast-on stitch is the first stitch at the tip of the left needle. Insert the right needle, knitwise, into that stitch, bring the yarn from the bottom of the needle to the top, wrap it around the right needle, and knit the stitch in the usual manner. Make sure you knit this stitch tightly.

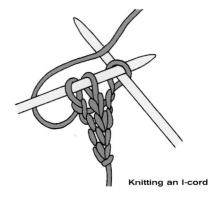

Knitting an I-cord

3. Knit the 2 remaining stitches on the needle.

4. Repeat steps 2 and 3 until the I-cord is the desired length.

## POMPOMS

These fuzzy balls can be as large or as small as you like. The following directions are for a standard size.

1. Cut a block of cardboard that is as wide as you want your pompom to be.

2. Wrap yarn around the cardboard 50–125 times, depending on the pompom's diameter and the yarn's weight. Keep the strands evenly spaced and don't overlap them too much in the center.

**Making a pompom or tassel:** Step 2

3. Insert an 8-inch (20cm) length of yarn through one side of the wrapped yarn. Draw in the ends of the short yarn and knot them together.

4. Slide the tip of your scissors under the yarn at the opposite edge and cut through all the layers.

5. Remove the cardboard and trim the yarn edges to neaten.

6. Thread the ends of the knot through a needle and pull them to the inside of the hat. Tie them in a square knot and weave in the loose ends.

**Making a pompom or tassel:** Steps 3 & 4

## TASSELS

The method for making tassels is similar to that for pompoms. Tassels can be as short or as long as you like.

1. Cut a block of cardboard that is the length you want your tassel to be.

2. Wrap yarn around the cardboard 25 times for worsted weight or 15 times for bulky weight.

3. Insert an 8-inch (20cm) length of yarn under one side of the wrapped yarn. Draw in the ends of the short yarn and knot them together.

4. Slide the tip of your scissors under the yarn at the opposite edge and cut through all the layers.

5. Wrap another 8-inch (20cm) length of yarn around the tassel ¾-inch (2cm) below the previous knot, tie it tightly, and let the ends blend into the rest of the tassel.

6. Cut the loose ends to the same length.

7. Thread the yarn ends for the upper knot through a yarn needle and pull both into position on the hat. Tie them in a square knot inside the hat. Weave in the loose ends.

# Carrot Top

Designed by Deb Gemmell, Cabin Fever

This project is for knitters who don't want to worry about testing gauge by making a swatch. The hat can be short (elf) or long (stocking). For an even longer version, knit more stripes. You needn't decide before you begin because the hat is knitted from the top down. The amount of yarn provided corresponds to the yarn weight used for the hat pictured; it may vary according to your own project. This hat was knit with yarn listed at right; you may use any yarn you choose because the gauge is determined as you knit.

**Level:** Easy!

**Sizes**

Personalized for baby, toddler, child, teen, or adult

**Finished circumferences**

Determined as you knit

**Yarn:** Brown Sheep Lamb's Pride Worsted
85% wool/15% mohair

**ELF:** 1 skein mc (rust), 1 skein cc A (autumn harvest), 1 skein cc B (sunburst gold), 1 skein cc C (spice)

**STOCKING:** 1 skein mc (rust), 1 skein cc A (autumn harvest), 1 skein cc B (sunburst gold), 1 skein cc C (spice)

**NOTE:** You can make this hat with any yarn weight. The elf (short) hat works up really fast in chunky yarn. A hat made from a lighter weight yarn has more flop.

**Needles**

One set #4 (3.5mm) dp needles

One #4 (3.5mm) circular needle, 16" (40cm) long

**Gauge**

Do not test gauge before starting this project

**Other supplies**

Ruler, stitch marker, yarn needle

---

**cc** = contrasting color ◆ **cont** = continue ◆ **dp** = double pointed ◆ **inc** = increase ◆ **K** = knit
**M1** = make 1 ◆ **mc** = main color ◆ **rnd(s)** = round(s) ◆ **st(s)** = stitch(es)

| KNITTING THE I-CORD TOPKNOT | ELF | STOCKING |
|---|---|---|
| With dp needles and mc, cast on | 4 sts | 4 sts |
| Using only two needles, make an I-cord for 1½" (4cm) or 5" (12.5cm) if you want to tie a knot in the cord. (See I-cord instructions on page 16.) | | |
| **INCREASING FOR TOP OF CROWN** | | |
| Round 1 (start of stripe): *K1, M1; repeat from * to end of rnd, place stitch marker on needle. (Slip marker to end of each new rnd as completed.) You will have | 8 sts | 8 sts |
| Round 2: Distribute sts on three dp needles and knit to end of rnd. | | |
| Knit for | 1" (2.5cm) | 1" (2.5cm) |
| Last Round Stripe 1: *K1, M1; repeat from * to end of rnd. You will have | 16 sts | 16 sts |
| Stripe 2: With cc A, knit to end of rnd. | | |
| From beginning of new stripe, knit for | 1" (2.5cm) | 1" (2.5cm) |
| Last Round Stripe 2: Repeat from * (see column at right) to end of rnd. | *K1, M1 | *K2, M1 |
| You will have | 32 sts | 24 sts |
| Stripe 3: With cc B, knit to end of rnd. | | |
| From beginning of new stripe, knit for | 1" (2.5cm) | 1" (2.5cm) |
| **NOTE:** If you're making a hat for a baby or small child, skip to "Gauging the Circumference" on the facing page. | | |
| Last Round Stripe 3: Repeat from * (see column at right) to end of rnd. | *K2, M1 | *K3, M1 |
| You will have | 48 sts | 32 sts |
| Stripe 4: With cc A, knit to end of rnd. | | |
| From beginning of new stripe, knit for | 1" (2.5cm) | 1" (2.5cm) |
| Last Round Stripe 4: Repeat from * to end of rnd. | *K3, M1 | K4, M1 |
| You will have | 64 sts | 40 sts |

| GAUGING THE CIRCUMFERENCE | ELF | STOCKING |
|---|---|---|
| Place hat flat on table. Using a section that doesn't have any inc, count the number of sts in 1" (2.5cm) of a rnd. This is your gauge. | | |
| Measure the head of the person who will wear the hat. (See page 8 for average head sizes.) | | |
| Multiply the head size by the gauge. For example, an average adult size needs 110¼ sts if you knit 5¼ sts to 1". Here's the calculation:<br>21" (53.5cm) x 5¼ sts = 110¼ sts. | | |
| Round fractions in the final st count. (In the example above, you round the st count to 110). This is the number of sts you need to have at the brim for the hat to fit the wearer. **NOTE:** A baby hat needs to be slightly shorter. Try it on the baby to determine suitable depth. | | |
| **ADJUSTING THE FIT** | | |
| Cont making stripes, inc sts on the last row of each color (when the stripe is 1"/2.5cm deep). With every inc rnd, knit 1 more st before the M1 inc, as established in "Increasing for Top of Crown." Change to circular needle when dp needles are crowded. | | |
| When as close as possible to number of sts needed for head circumference (without exceeding that number), in the next stripe inc evenly in rnd to exact number you worked out above. For example: When hat reaches 96 sts, in next stripe inc 14 sts for 110 sts in rnd. | | |
| **ADDING DEPTH AND BRIM** | | |
| Cont knitting 1" color stripes, without inc rnds, for | 4" (10cm) | 3" (7.5cm) |
| Change yarn color for brim, knit 2" (5cm) for rolled edge. Cast off. | | |
| **FINISHING** | | |
| Weave in loose ends, using technique on page 14 to hide color "jogs" visible at the end of rnds where stripes change color. At brim, place ends on right (knit) side so invisible when rolled to finished position. | | |

# Watch Cap

Designed by Melinda Goodfellow, Yankee Knitter Designs

This hat is knitted flat on straight needles in stockinette stitch, then seamed. Stockinette stitch is the classic technique of knitting on one side and purling on the other. The pictured hat is knit with worsted yarn listed at right, but the pattern includes directions for bulky yarn too; you may use any yarn that will provide the required gauge.

**bw** = bulky weight ◆ **K** = knit
**K2tog** = knit 2 stitches together ◆ **P** = purl
**st(s)** = stitch(es) ◆ **St st** = stockinette st
**ww** = worsted weight

## Notes for charts on pages 24–25

In columns 2, 3, and 4, the first number is the end-of-row stitch count for worsted-weight yarn; the second number is the stitch count for bulky-weight yarn. When only one set of numbers is given, it refers to both weights of yarn.

**Level:** Easy!

### Sizes and finished circumferences

Child, 19" (48cm); Adult medium, 20" (51cm); Adult large, 21" (53cm)

### Worsted Yarn Version (pictured)

Brown Sheep Prairie Silk 10% silk/18% mohair/72% wool

2 skeins treasury turquoise

### Needles for worsted version

One pair #7 (4.5mm) straight needles *or size needed to obtain gauge*

One pair #6 (4mm) straight needles *or one size smaller than larger needles*

### Gauge for worsted version

20 sts = 4" (10cm) on #7 (4.5mm) needles in St st, before blocking

### Bulky Yarn Version

**Child:** 85 yds
**Adult M:** 110 yds
**Adult L:** 120 yds

### Needles for bulky version

One pair #10 (6mm) straight needles *or size needed to obtain gauge*

One pair #9 (5.5mm) straight needles *or one size smaller than larger needles*

### Gauge for bulky version

14 sts = 4" (10cm) on #10 (6mm) needles in St st, before blocking

### Other supplies

Cardboard (optional, for pompom), yarn needle

| KNITTING THE BRIM (Both Yarns) | CHILD | ADULT M | ADULT L |
|---|---|---|---|
| | WW/BW | WW/BW | WW/BW |
| With larger needles, cast on<br>NOTE: Cast on with the larger needles, then switch to the smaller set. Casting on too tightly is a common problem, and this ensures that your brim won't be too snug. | 94/66 sts | 100/70 sts | 106/74 sts |
| Row 1: Change to smaller needles, *K1, P1; repeat from * to end of row. | | | |
| Repeat Row 1 (K1, P1 ribbing) for | 3" (7.5cm) | 3½" (9cm) | 3½" (9cm) |
| **KNITTING THE HAT** (Both Yarns) | | | |
| Change back to larger needles and work in St st for | 4" (10cm) | 5" (13cm) | 6" (15cm) |
| End with purl row completed. | | | |
| **DECREASING FOR CROWN** (Worsted Only) | | | |
| NOTE: For bulky hat, skip this section. Row 1: *K10, K2tog; repeat from * to end of row, knit any remaining sts. You'll have | 87 sts | 92 sts | 98 sts |
| Rows 2 and 4: Purl. | | | |
| Row 3: *K9, K2tog; repeat from * to end of row, knit any remaining sts. You'll have | 80 sts | 84 sts | 90 sts |
| **DECREASING FOR CROWN** (Both Yarns) | | | |
| NOTE: The bulky hat starts here. Row 5: *K8, K2tog; repeat from * to end of row, knit any remaining sts. You'll have | 72/60 sts | 76/63 sts | 81/67 sts |
| Rows 6, 8, 10, 12, 14, 16, and 18: Purl. | | | |
| Row 7: *K7, K2tog; repeat from * to end of row, knit any remaining sts. You'll have | 64/54 sts | 68/56 sts | 72/60 sts |
| Row 9: *K6, K2tog; repeat from * to end of row, knit any remaining sts. You'll have | 56/48 sts | 60/49 sts | 63/53 sts |

| | CHILD | ADULT M | ADULT L |
|---|---|---|---|
| | WW/BW | WW/BW | WW/BW |
| Row 11: *K5, K2tog; repeat from * to end of row, knit any remaining sts. You'll have | 48/42 sts | 52/42 sts | 54/46 sts |
| Row 13: *K4, K2tog; repeat from * to end of row, knit any remaining sts. You'll have | 40/35 sts | 44/35 sts | 45/38 sts |
| Row 15: *K3, K2tog; repeat from * to end of row, knit any remaining sts. You'll have | 32/28 sts | 36/28 sts | 36/31 sts |
| Row 17: *K2, K2tog; repeat from * to end of row, knit any remaining sts. You'll have | 24/21 sts | 27/21 sts | 27/24 sts |
| Row 19: *K1, K2tog; repeat from * to end of row, knit any remaining sts. You'll have | 16/14 sts | 18/14 sts | 18/16 sts |
| Row 20: *P2tog; repeat from * to end of row, purl any remaining sts. Cut yarn. You'll have | 8/7 sts | 9/7 sts | 9/8 sts |
| **FINISHING THE HAT** | | | |
| Draw yarn through remaining sts and pull tight. | | | |
| Above the ribbing, sew seam with right (knit) sides together. | | | |
| Sew seam for ribbed band with wrong side together so the seam is hidden when ribbing is turned up 1" (2.5cm) to its finished position. | | | |
| Weave in loose ends. | | | |
| **MAKING THE POMPOM** (Optional) | | | |
| See page 17 for detailed instructions on making a pompom. | | | |
| Large pompom: Wrap yarn around 3½" (9cm) cardboard square 125 times for worsted yarn or 75 times for bulky yarn. | | | |
| Small pompom: Wrap yarn around 2½" (6cm) cardboard square 85 times for worsted yarn or 50 times for bulky yarn. | | | |
| Complete pompom and sew to top of hat. | | | |

# Three-in-One

Designed by Nancy Lindberg

This pattern offers three versions of headwarmers. Start by making a headband, perfect to wear for vigorous outdoor activity when a hat is too warm. Add a cap to the headband and you have a classic-style hat. Add earflaps to make a helmet, which will keep you toasty on cold and windy days. The hat pictured was knit with yarn listed at right; you may use any yarn that will provide the required gauge.

### Sizes and finished circumferences
Child, 18" (46cm); Adult medium, 20" (51cm); Adult large, 22" (56cm)

**Yarn for headband:** Brown Sheep Lamb's Pride worsted, 85% wool/15% mohair

1 skein mc (deep charcoal)

1 skein cc A (lotus pink)

**Yarn for hat or helmet:** Brown Sheep Lamb's Pride worsted, 85% wool/15% mohair

2 skeins mc (deep charcoal)

1 skein cc A (lotus pink)

5 yds cc B (emerald fantasy)

10 yds cc C (dynamite blue)

5 yds cc D (limeade)

### Needles
One #6 (4mm) circular needle, 16" (40cm) long, *or size needed to obtain gauge*

One #8 (5mm) circular needle, 16" (40cm) long, *or two sizes larger than smaller needle*

### Gauge
20 sts = 4" (10cm) on #8 (5mm) in St st, before blocking

### Other supplies
2–3" (5–7.5cm) cardboard square (optional, for pompom), stitch marker, yarn needle

---

**cc** = contrast color ◆ **cont** = continue **inc** = increase ◆ **K** = knit ◆ **K2tog** = knit 2 stitches together ◆ **M1** = make 1 ◆ **mc** = main color ◆ **P** = purl ◆ **P2tog** = purl 2 stitches together (applies to other numbers as well) ◆ **rnd(s)** = round(s) ◆ **ssk** = slip, slip, knit 2 stitches together ◆ **st(s)** = stitch(es) ◆ **St st** = stockinette stitch

| GETTING STARTED *(Headband, Hat, and Helmet)* | CHILD | ADULT M | ADULT L |
|---|---|---|---|
| With #6 (4mm) needle and mc, cast on | 80 sts | 90 sts | 100 sts |
| Place stitch marker. Join rnd, being careful not to twist sts. (Slip marker to end of each new rnd as completed.) | | | |
| Rounds 1–3: Purl. | | | |
| Round 4: Knit, inc 1 st (M1) after every | 8th st | 9th st | 10th st |
| You will have | 90 sts | 100 sts | 110 sts |
| Change to #8 (5mm) needle. | | | |
| Next rnd(s) (headband only): Knit | 1 rnd | 3 rnds | 3 rnds |
| Next rnds (hat and helmet only): Knit | 3 rnds | 3 rnds | 3 rnds |
| KNITTING PATTERN *(Headband, Hat, and Helmet)* | | | |
| Join cc A. | | | |
| Knitting ALL rnds, work the pattern by following the chart of choice (excluding "Chart for Crown") on page 31. Read each rnd from right to left, starting with line 1 at the bottom. | | | |
| Repeat 10-st pattern to end of rnd, then work line 2 to end of next rnd. Cont in this manner until chart is finished. | | | |
| Cut cc A. | | | |
| If you are making a hat or helmet, go to "Continuing for Hat and Helmet" on the facing page. | | | |
| DECREASING *(Headband only)* | | | |
| With mc, knit | 1 rnd | 3 rnds | 3 rnds |
| Decrease Round: Repeat from * (see column at right) to end of rnd. | *K7, K2tog | *K8, K2tog | *K9, K2tog |
| You will have | 80 sts | 90 sts | 100 sts |
| With #6 (4mm) needle, purl | 3 rnds | 3 rnds | 3 rnds |
| Cast off using purl sts. Weave yarn ends on wrong (purl) side. | | | |

| CONTINUING  (Hat and Helmet) | CHILD | ADULT M | ADULT L |
|---|---|---|---|
| Rounds 1–4: With #8 (5mm) needle and mc, knit. | | | |
| Rounds 5–7: Purl. | | | |
| Rounds 8–11: Knitting ALL rnds, work "Chart for Crown" on page 31. Read each rnd from right to left, starting with line 1 at the bottom. Repeat 5-st pattern to end of rnd, then work line 2 to end of next rnd. Cont in this manner until chart is finished. | | | |
| Repeat "Chart for Crown" on page 31 until piece from beginning of headband measures | 7" (18cm) | 7.5" (19cm) | 8" (20cm) |
| **DECREASING FOR CROWN**  (Hat and Helmet) | | | |
| Round 1: *K3, K2tog; repeat from * to end of rnd. You will have | 64 sts | 72 sts | 80 sts |
| Round 2: *K2, K2tog; repeat from * to end of rnd. You will have | 48 sts | 54 sts | 60 sts |
| Round 3: *K1, K2tog; repeat from * to end of rnd. You will have | 32 sts | 36 sts | 40 sts |
| If you are making the hat only, go to "Finishing" on page 30. | | | |
| **KNITTING RIGHT EARFLAP**  (Helmet only) | | | |
| Row 1: Measure along cast-on edge 1½" (4cm) from center back. Pick up | 20 sts | 22 sts | 24 sts |
| With mc, knit to end. | | | |
| Row 2: K3, purl to last 3 sts, K3. | | | |
| Row 3: P3, knit to last 3 sts, P3. | | | |
| Row 4: K3, purl to last 3 sts, K3. | | | |
| Row 5: P3, ssk, knit to last 5 sts, K2tog, P3. | | | |
| Rows 6–9: Repeat Rows 2–5. You will have | 16 sts | 18 sts | 20 sts |
| Repeat Rows 4 and 5 until 8 sts remain, ending with a wrong side row completed. | | | |
| Next row: P3tog, P2tog, P3tog. You will have | 3 sts | 3 sts | 3 sts |

| KNITTING LEFT EARFLAP (Helmet only) | CHILD | ADULT M | ADULT L |
|---|---|---|---|
| Measure along front cast-on edge from first earflap | 7"(17.5cm) | 7.5"(19cm) | 8"(20cm) |
| With mc, pick up and knit | 20 sts | 22 sts | 24 sts |
| Work same as right earflap. | | | |
| **FINISHING** (Hat and Helmet) | | | |
| To make an I-cord, join cc C with remaining 3 sts. Make 3" I-cord (see I-cord instructions on page 16). Cut yarn. Thread yarn end on needle and pull through sts to tighten. Pull loose end inside I-cord and weave in to secure. | | | |
| To attach a pompom, draw remaining sts as tightly as possible (there will be a hole in the center). Pull loose end to wrong (purl) side and weave in ends. Sew closed the hole in the top of the crown. Make and attach a pompom (see pompom instructions on page 17). | | | |
| Cut yarn ends, thread ends on yarn needle, and thread through remaining sts. | | | |

# Three-in-One Charts

## CHART FOR CROWN

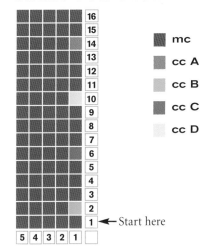

- ■ mc
- ■ cc A
- ■ cc B
- ■ cc C
- ■ cc D

## SNOWFLAKE

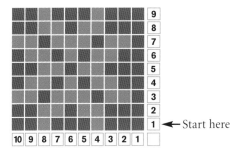

## SHAMROCK

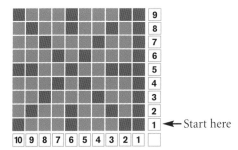

## HEART

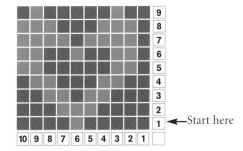

## DIAMOND

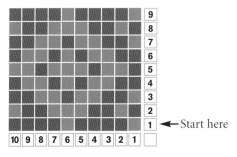

## ARROW

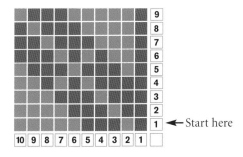

# Slip-a-Color

Designed by Lynda Gemmell, Cabin Fever

This hat is quick and colorful and one size fits most adults. It's a great project in which to learn an easy slip stitch and experiment with color. The slip-stitch technique gives the effect of a two-color pattern while using only one color per round. In short order, you will have a vibrant hat knit in the round. The hat pictured was knit with yarn listed at right; you may use any yarn that will provide the required gauge.

**Level:** Easy!

**Size and finished circumference**

Adult medium, 21½" (55cm)

**Yarn:** Brown Sheep Lamb's Pride worsted, 85% wool/15% mohair

1 skein mc (amethyst)

1 skein cc A (fuschia)

1 skein cc B (sunburst gold)

1 skein cc C (red baron)

> **NOTE:** 2.5g/5 yds is enough yarn for one stripe (2 rounds of slip-stitch pattern)

**Needles**

One #6 (4mm) circular needle, 16" (40cm) long, *or size needed to obtain gauge*

One #8 (5mm) circular needle, 16" (40cm) long, *or size needed to obtain gauge*

**Gauge**

20 sts = 4" (10cm) in sl st pattern on #8 (5mm) needles and 20 sts = 4" (10cm) in St st on #6 (4mm) needle, before blocking

**Other supplies**

Stitch marker, yarn needle

---

**cc** = contrast color  ◆  **cont** = continue  ◆  **dec** = decrease  ◆  **K** = knit  ◆  **K2tog** = knit 2 stitches together  ◆  **mc** = main color  ◆  **P** = purl  ◆  **rnd(s)** = round(s)  ◆  **sl** = slip
**sl st** = slip stitch  ◆  **st(s)** = stitch(es)  ◆  **St st** = stockinette stitch

## KNITTING THE BRIM

Using #6 needle and mc, cast on 108 sts. Place stitch marker at end of rnd. Join rnd, being careful not to twist sts. (Slip marker to end of each new rnd as completed.)

Knit for 3" (7.5cm).

Last Round: Change to #8 needle and cc A; knit to end of rnd.

## KNITTING THE PATTERN

Round 1: With cc B, *K1, sl1 purlwise; repeat from * to end of rnd. You will still have 108 sts.

Round 2: With cc B, *P1, sl1; repeat from * to end of rnd.

Round 3: With cc A, knit to end of rnd.

Round 4: Change to cc C, *sl1, K1; repeat from * to end of rnd.

Round 5: With cc C, *sl1, P1; repeat from * to end of rnd.

Round 6: With cc A, knit to end of rnd.

Repeat Rounds 1–6 for 5" (13cm), changing to cc B or cc C on Round 1 or Rounds 1 & 4.

## DECREASING FOR CROWN

Round 1: With #6 needle and mc, *K16, K2tog; repeat from * to end of rnd. You will have 102 sts.

# Successful Slipping

Moving a stitch from one needle to another is a fairly simple matter, yet you can do a few things to make the finished effect look even better. In this pattern, for example, you need to slip the stitch purlwise. Here's how it's done:

1. Keeping the yarn at the back of the work, insert your right needle into the next stitch on the left needle as if you were going to purl it.

2. Slide the stitch onto the right needle without working it.

3. As you make the next stitch, take care that you don't draw the yarn too tightly.

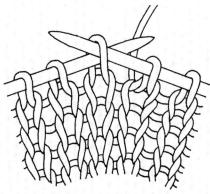

**Slipping a stitch purlwise**

Round 2: *K15, K2tog; repeat from * to end of rnd. You will have 96 sts.

Round 3: *K14, K2tog; repeat from * to end of rnd. You will have 90 sts.

Cont to dec every rnd, knitting 1 less st between each K2tog, until 30 sts remain, or until you can no longer stretch the sts around the needle.

## FINISHING THE HAT

Cut yarn. Using yarn needle, thread end through sts on needle and pull tightly to close top of hat. Weave all loose ends through sts on wrong (inside) of hat. At brim, sew ends on right side so invisible when rolled to finish position.

## Colorful Colorways

This is a great pattern to try if you're thinking about experimenting with a variety of color combinations and you want to use up odd balls of yarn. You could knit the brim and upper crown in the main color or try a different color for each. Or use the background color for the pattern background and one or two contrast colors for the slip-stitch pattern. Once you are comfortable with the pattern, try changing the background color every time you alter one of the slip-stitch yarns, or leave the background constant and work the slip stitch entirely in one color.

# Color Me Bright

Designed by Deb and Lynda Gemmell, Cabin Fever

You can use odds and ends of chunky wool from your yarn basket to make this warm, colorful hat. In this project, natural-color wool is dyed with Kool-Aid to give this basic toque a bright and funky look. The I-cord tails that decorate the top of the hat are approximately 2 inches long, but you can knit them as long (or as short) as you like. You could even make them *very* long and sew bells on the ends or tie them into knots.

**cc** = contrast color ♦ **dp** = double pointed
**K** = knit ♦ **K2tog** = knit 2 stitches together
**mc** = main color ♦ **rnd(s)** = round(s)
**st(s)** = stitch(es) ♦ **St st** = stockinette stitch

**Level:** Easy!

**Sizes and finished circumferences**

Baby, 16" (41cm); Child, 18" (46cm)

**Yarn:** Chunky-weight 100% wool

> **Baby:** 1 skein mc (heather blue) and 1 skein (white or natural) for all ccs
>
> **Child:** 1 skein mc (heather blue) and 1 skein (white or natural) for all ccs
>
> NOTE: You can use double-knitting or sport-weight yarn for this hat. Simply double the yardage and knit the entire hat with two strands worked as one. Two strands of double-knit or sport-weight wool are the equivalent of one strand of chunky-weight wool.

**Needles**

One US #10 (6mm) circular needle, 16" (40cm) long, *or size needed to obtain gauge*
One set US #10 (6mm) dp needles *or same size used in circular needle*

**Gauge**

14 sts = 4" (10cm) in St st, before blocking

**Dyeing equipment**

Teakettle, medium-size saucepan, four packets unsweetened Kool-Aid, 2 cups white vinegar, metal spoon, plastic hangers

**Other supplies**

Stitch holder, yarn needle

| KNITTING THE ROLLED BRIM | BABY | CHILD |
|---|---|---|
| Using mc and circular needle, cast on | 56 sts | 64 sts |
| Join rnd, being careful not to twist sts. | | |
| Knit to length you prefer for rolled brim or | 1¼" (3cm) | 1¾"(4.5cm) |
| **KNITTING THE PATTERN** | | |
| Knit the pattern, following the chart on the facing page. Read each rnd from right to left, starting with line 1 at the bottom. Repeat the 4-st pattern to end of rnd, then work line 2 to end of next rnd. Continue in this manner until chart is finished. Change the cc as indicated. This pattern shows four ccs, but you can use as many ccs as you wish. | | |
| **DECREASING FOR THE CROWN** | | |
| Using mc, decrease for the crown. Rounds 1 and 2: Knit. | | |
| Round 3: *K6, K2tog; repeat from * to end of rnd. You will have | 49 sts | 56 sts |
| Round 4: Knit. Change to dp needles. | | |
| Round 5: *K5, K2tog; repeat from * to end of rnd. You will have | 42 sts | 48 sts |
| Round 6: Knit. | | |
| Round 7: *K2tog; repeat from * until you have | 12 sts | 12 sts |
| **KNITTING THE I-CORD TAILS** | | |
| With the 12 sts remaining, knit four I-cord tails, using one cc for each tail. Only two dp needles are needed for this technique. (See I-cord instructions on page 16 for more information.) | | |
| Round 1: Slip first 3 sts on a dp needle; place remaining sts on stitch holder. With one cc, K3. | | |
| Round 2: *Slide the 3 sts to the other end of the needle, K1 by pulling yarn from last st up to first st and knit tightly, K2. | | |

| | BABY | CHILD |
|---|---|---|
| Repeat last rnd 9 more times (or to desired length). Cast off 3 I-cord sts. | | |
| With another cc, slip 3 more sts on dp needle; make another I-cord, following the directions for the first one. Make two more tails with remaining sts. | | |
| At brim, sew ends on right side so invisible when brim rolled to position. | | |

## Kool-Aid Dyeing

1. Divide white or natural-color 100% wool into two or three lots, depending on the number of colors you want. Wind each lot around your hand to form a small skein. Using wool, tie the skein *loosely* in one or two places to keep the yarn from tangling.
2. Wet the wool completely in cool water and set aside.
3. Fill a large teakettle with water and bring to a boil. Pour enough boiling water into a medium-size saucepan so that it will cover the wool. Don't put the wool in the water yet.
4. Add one packet of Kool-Aid and ⅓–½ cup white vinegar to the water in the saucepan and stir with a metal spoon to create the dye liquid.
5. Quickly immerse a small, wet skein in the dye, adding more water if necessary so the wool is completely covered. Leave it in the dye for about 1 minute, or simmer on the stovetop until the water is clear.
6. Remove the wool from the dye and rinse in cool water. Hang on a plastic hanger to dry.
7. Discard the used liquid and repeat the dyeing process for each color.

**COLOR ME BRIGHT CHART**

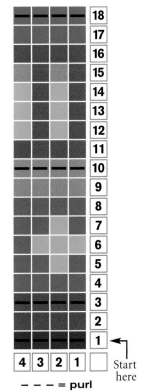

— — — = purl

# Three-Gauge Beret

Designed by Nancy Lindberg

This classic beret never goes out of style, and the directions allow you to knit it in three weights of yarn. The heavy-weight gauge is quite nice in mohair, but experiment and find the yarn that is just right for the look you want. The hats pictured here and on page 43 were knit with yarns listed at right; you may use any yarn that will provide the required gauge.

---

**dec** = decrease ◆ **dp** = double pointed
**inc** = increase ◆ **K** = knit ◆ **K2tog** =
knit 2 sitches together ◆ **rnd(s)** =
round(s) ◆ **st**(s) = stitch(es) ◆ **St st** =
stockinette stitch ◆ **YO** = yarn over

---

**Level:** Easy!
**Size and finished circumference**
One size, 19" (48cm)

## Sport-Weight Version

100g/250 yds
**Needles for sport-weight version**
#4 (3.5mm) and #6 (4mm) circular needles,
    16" (40cm) long, *or size needed to obtain gauge*
One set #6 (4mm) dp needles *or size needed to obtain gauge*
**Gauge for sport-weight version**
24 sts = 4" (10cm) on larger needles in St st

## Worsted-Weight Version (page 43)

2 skeins periwinkle Brown Sheep Lamb's Pride
**Needles for worsted-weight version**
#6 (4mm) and #8 (5mm) circular needles,
    16" (40cm) long, *or size needed to obtain gauge*
One set #8 (5mm) dp needles *or size needed to obtain gauge*
**Gauge for worsted-weight version**
20 sts = 4" (10cm) on larger needles in St st

## Heavy-Weight Version (facing page)

1 skein #6599 Classic Elite La Gran Mohair
**Needles for heavy-weight version**
#7 (4.5mm) and #9 (5.5mm) circular needles,
    16" (40cm) long, *or size needed to obtain gauge*
One set #9 (5.5mm) dp needles *or size needed to obtain gauge*
**Gauge for heavy-weight version**
16 sts = 4" (10cm) on larger needles in St st
**Other supplies**
Stitch marker, yarn needle

| KNITTING THE CUFF | SPORT | WORSTED | HEAVY |
|---|---|---|---|
| Using smaller circular needle, cast on | 114 sts | 94 sts | 76 sts |
| Place stitch marker at end of 1st rnd. Join rnd, being careful not to twist sts. (Slip marker to end of each new rnd as completed.) | | | |
| Knit every rnd for | 2" (5cm) | 2" (5cm) | 2" (5cm) |
| Picot edge: *YO, K2tog repeat from * to end of rnd. | | | |
| From picot edge, knit in rnds for | 2" (5cm) | 2" (5cm) | 2" (5cm) |
| **BUILDING THE SIDES** | | | |
| Next (inc) Round: Knit, working evenly spaced inc of | 62 sts | 50 sts | 36 sts |
| Sts on needle at end of inc rnd: | 176 sts | 144 sts | 112 sts |
| Change to larger circular needle | 6 (4mm) | 8 (5mm) | 9 (5.5mm) |
| From inc rnd, continue in St st for | 4" (10cm) | 4" (10cm) | 4" (10cm) |
| **DECREASING FOR THE CROWN** | | | |
| Round 1: Repeat from * (see column at right) to end of rnd. | *K20, K2tog | *K16, K2tog | *K12, K2tog |
| Sts on needle at end of rnd | 168 sts | 136 sts | 104 sts |
| Rounds 2, 4, and 6: Knit. | | | |
| Round 3: Repeat from * (see column at right) to end of rnd. | *K19, K2tog | *K15, K2tog | *K11, K2tog |
| Sts on needle at end of rnd | 160 sts | 128 sts | 96 sts |
| Round 5: Repeat from * (see column at right) to end of rnd. | *K18, K2tog | *K14, K2tog | *K10, K2tog |
| Sts on needle at end of rnd | 152 sts | 120 sts | 88 sts |
| Continue dec every other rnd in established pattern until 16 sts remain. Transfer to dp needles when circular is too long. | | | |

| FINISHING THE HAT | SPORT | WORSTED | HEAVY |
|---|---|---|---|
| Cut yarn. | | | |
| Thread end onto yarn needle, then draw end through sts and weave in on wrong (purl) side of work. | | | |
| Fold hem along picot edge and tack cast-on edge inside beret. | | | |

# Pillbox Flowers

Designed by Deb Gemmell, Cabin Fever

This quick project is very versatile. Try knitting it with several colors or as a knit/purl pattern. The hat starts with an I-cord tail that is increased in eight sections to make a flat crown. Because it is knit from the top down, the length can be adjusted as you go. Some people like their hats to sit at the top of their ears; others prefer their ears covered. For a longer version, include additional rounds before and/or after the graph. The hat pictured was knit with yarn listed at right; you may use any yarn that will provide the required gauge.

**Size and finished circumference**

Adult medium–large, 24" (60cm)

**Yarn:** Classic Elite Montera 50% llama/50% wool
2 skeins mc (dark seafoam/#3872) and 1 skein cc (celery/#3887)

**Needles**

One set #7 (4.5mm) dp needles *or size needed to obtain gauge*

One #6 (4mm) circular needle, 16" (40cm) long, *or one size smaller than larger needles* (optional, for ribbed edge)

**Gauge**

20 sts = 4" (10cm) on #7 (4.5mm) needles in St st, before blocking

**Other supplies**

Eight stitch markers (use one stitch marker in an alternate color), yarn needle

---

**cc** = contrast color ◆ **cont** = continue
**dp** = double pointed ◆ **inc** = increase
**K** = knit ◆ **K2tog** = knit 2 stitches together
**M1** = make 1 ◆ **mc** = main color
**rnd(s)** = round(s) ◆ **st(s)** = stitch(es)
**St st** = stockinette stitch

## STARTING WITH THE I-CORD

With mc and two dp needles, cast on 4 sts. Knit a 1"-long I-cord (see directions on page 16).

## INCREASING FOR CROWN

The crown is a wheel divided into eight sections. You will be increasing 8 sts every second rnd.

Round 1: With two dp needles to hold sts and a third needle to knit, *K1, M1; repeat from * to end of rnd. You will have 8 sts.

All even-number Rounds: Knit.

Round 3: *K1, M1; repeat from * to end of rnd. Redistribute sts on three dp needles. You will have 16 sts.

Round 5: *K2, M1; repeat from * to end of rnd. You will have 24 sts.

Round 7: *K3, M1; repeat from * to end of rnd. You will have 32 sts.

Round 9: *K4, M1, place marker; repeat from * to end of rnd, using marker in alternate color for end of rnd. You will have 40 sts.

Slip markers up to new row as you knit even-number rnds. On every odd-number rnd, cont to inc 1 st at the end of each section (M1 before marker), until you have a total of 128 sts on the needle (16 sts in each section). Change to the circular needle when sts are crowded.

## Ribbed Cuff

If you wish, you can make ribbing for the bottom edge instead of the I-cord rim. The ribbing gives you a slightly longer hat and provides a more flexible border.

Using the main color, change to #6 (4mm) circular needle. Knit one round. In second round, *K2, K2tog; repeat from * to last 2 stitches; K2tog. You will have 94 stitches. Work in K1, P1 ribbing for 1". Cast off in rib.

## KNITTING THE HAT

Round 1: Knit.

Rounds 2–4: Purl.

Round 5: Knit.

Round 6: K2tog, K62, K2tog, knit to end of rnd. You will have 126 sts.

## KNITTING THE PATTERN

Knit the pattern, following the chart at right. Read each rnd from right to left, starting with line 1 at the bottom. Repeat 14-st pattern to end of rnd, then work line 2 to end of next rnd. Cont in this manner until chart is finished.

## KNITTING THE I-CORD RIM

Rounds 1 and 2: With mc, knit.

Round 3: *K2, K2tog; repeat from * to last 2 sts, K2. You will have 95 sts.

Round 4: Still with mc, cast on 3 sts on left (next) needle.

*K2, K2tog through back loops of sts. Slip 3 sts back onto the left needle; repeat from * along the edge of hat to end of rnd, cast off last 3 sts.

## FINISHING THE HAT

Sew together ends of I-cord. Weave loose ends through sts on inside of hat.

PILLBOX FLOWERS CHART

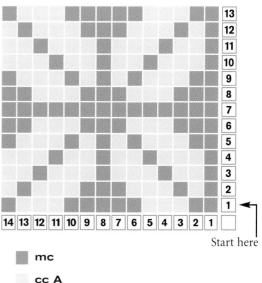

Start here

mc

cc A

47

# Bunnies and Carrots

Designed by Barbara Telford, Woodsmoke Woolworks

This adorable hat comes in three sizes and is knit in the round on double-pointed needles. Basic crocheting is also required, but don't worry – you only need to make a simple chain stitch, and you'll find instructions on page 55. The hat pictured was knit with yarn listed at right; you may use any yarn that will provide the required gauge. Because ties on children's hats can be dangerous, the drawstrings attached to the earflaps are recommended only for adults' hats.

## Sizes and finished circumferences

Toddler, 16" (40cm); Kid, 17½" (45cm); Adult medium, 19" (48cm)

**Yarn:** Briggs & Little Regal 100% wool
1 skein mc (blue)
1 skein cc A (light blue)
1 skein cc B (white)
1 skein cc C (orange)
1 skein cc D (green)
1 skein cc E (brown)

## Needles

One set #7 (4.5mm) dp needles *or size needed to obtain gauge*
One set #4 (3.5mm) straight needles *or three sizes smaller than dp needles*
One #7 (4.5mm) crochet hook

## Gauge

20 sts = 4" (10cm) on #7 (4.5 mm) needles in St st, before blocking

## Other supplies

Two spare needles, stitch marker, stuffing for carrot tassels, yarn needle

**cc** = contrast color ◆ **cont** = continue ◆ **inc** = increase ◆ **K** = knit ◆ **K2tog** = knit 2 stitches together (also applies to other numbers) ◆ **mc** = main color ◆ **P** = purl
**P2tog** = purl 2 stitches together ◆ **pu** = pick up ◆ **rnd(s)** = round(s) **st(s)** = stitch(es)
**St st** = stockinette stitch ◆ **YO** = yarn over

| KNITTING THE EARFLAPS | TODDLER | KID | ADULT M |
|---|---|---|---|
| Using mc and #7 (4.5mm) needles, cast on | 3 sts | 3 sts | 3 sts |
| Rows 1, 3, and 5: Purl. | | | |
| Row 2: K1, inc 2 sts in next st, K1. You will have | 5 sts | 5 sts | 5 sts |
| Row 4: K1, inc 1 st in next st, K1, inc 1 st in next st, K1. You will have | 7 sts | 7 sts | 7 sts |
| Row 6: K1, inc 1 st in next st, knit to last 2 sts, inc 1 st in next st, K1. You will have | 9 sts | 9 sts | 9 sts |
| Row 7: Purl. | | | |
| Repeat Rows 6 and 7 until row has | 23 sts | 23 sts | 27 sts |
| End with knit row completed. Place on spare needle. | | | |
| Make another earflap in the same manner. | | | |
| KNITTING THE HAT | | | |
| Using mc and #7 (4.5mm) circular needles, cast on | 80 sts | 88 sts | 96 sts |
| Evenly divide sts on three #7 (4.5mm) needles. Join rnd, being careful not to twist sts. Place stitch marker at end of rnd. (Slip marker to end of each new rnd as completed.) | 26, 28, 26 sts per needle | 28, 32, 28 sts per needle | 32, 32, 32 per needle |
| Rounds 1–3: Knit. | | | |
| ATTACHING THE FLAPS | | | |
| Round 1: Place marker. Knit 3 sts, place wrong (purl) side of one earflap on wrong side of hat, knit together next st of hat with first st of flap as if 1 st (see illustration on page 55). | | | |
| Cont joining flap to hat with next | 22 sts | 22 sts | 26 sts |
| Knit | 28 sts | 32 sts | 32 sts |
| Join remaining earflap to next | 23 sts | 23 sts | 27 sts |

| | TODDLER | KID | ADULT M |
|---|---|---|---|
| Knit to end of rnd. | | | |
| You will have | 80 sts | 88 sts | 96 sts |
| Knit | 2 rnds | 3 rnds | 5 rnds |
| **KNITTING THE PATTERN** | | | |
| Knit, following Border Chart on page 54. Read each rnd from right to left, starting with line 1 at the bottom. Repeat line 1 to end of rnd, then start line 2, again reading chart from right to left. Cont to end of chart. | | | |
| Work Bunny Chart on page 54, making a white bobble at every charted X. (See page 54 for instructions on making a bobble.) | | | |
| Work Border Chart again to complete color work. | | | |
| **DECREASING FOR THE CROWN** | | | |
| Rounds 1, 3, 5, 7, 9, 11, 13, and 15: Knit | 2 rnds | 3 rnds | 4 rnds |
| Round 2: *K6, K2tog; repeat from * to end of rnd. You will have | 70 sts | 84 sts | 84 sts |
| Round 4: *K5, K2tog; repeat from * to end of rnd. You will have | 60 sts | 72 sts | 72 sts |
| Round 6: *K4, K2tog; repeat from * to end of rnd. You will have | 50 sts | 60 sts | 60 sts |
| Round 8: *K3, K2tog; repeat from * to end of rnd. You will have | 40 sts | 48 sts | 48 sts |
| Round 10: *K2, K2tog; repeat from * to end of rnd. You will have | 30 sts | 36 sts | 36 sts |
| Round 12: *K1, K2tog; repeat from * to end of rnd. You will have | 20 sts | 24 sts | 24 sts |
| Round 14: K2tog to end of rnd. You will have | 10 sts | 12 sts | 12 sts |

| FINISHING THE HAT | TODDLER | KID | ADULT M |
|---|---|---|---|
| Cut yarn. | | | |
| Thread end onto yarn needle and pull the end through all sts remaining on knitting needle. While pulling yarn end to tighten sts, bring end through center, to inside of hat. | | | |
| Turn hat inside out and weave in all loose ends. | | | |
| **KNITTING THE CARROT TASSELS** | | | |
| Knit carrots in St st, knitting on odd rows, turning, and purling on even rows. See Carrot Chart on page 55 for guidance as you work the following increases and decreases. Using #4 (3.5mm) needles and cc C (orange), cast on | 4 sts | 4 sts | 4 sts |
| Rows 1 and 3: Knit. | | | |
| Rows 2 and 4: Purl. | | | |
| Row 5: Inc 1 st in each st to end of row. You will have | 8 sts | 8 sts | 8 sts |
| Row 6–8: Work in St st, starting with a purl row. | | | |
| Row 9: *Inc 1 st in next st, K1; repeat from * to end of row. You will have | 12 sts | 12 sts | 12 sts |
| Row 10–12: Work in St st, starting with a purl row. | | | |
| Row 13: *K1, inc 1 st in next st, K1; repeat from * to end of row. You will have | 16 sts | 16 sts | 16 sts |
| Rows 14–16: Work in St st, starting with a purl row. | | | |
| Row 17: K2tog to end of row. You will have | 8 sts | 8 sts | 8 sts |
| Row 18: *P2tog to end of row. You will have | 4 sts | 4 sts | 4 sts |

| | TODDLER | KID | ADULT M |
|---|---|---|---|
| Row 19 (leaf loops; see detail photo on page 55): Join cc D (green), *K1 (insert left needle in front loop of st on right needle, K1 starting with YO right needle) 16 times (like making a crocheted chain), with left needle pu cc C (orange) st at base of "chain," K1, pass cc D st on right needle over cc C st also on right needle; repeat from * to end of row. You will have | 4 sts | 4 sts | 4 sts |
| Cast off. | | | |
| Fold carrot in half vertically with right (knit) side inside. Sew edges together starting at top; sew almost to bottom, leaving a hole for stuffing. Turn carrot right side out, insert stuffing, and sew hole closed. Tuck ends of yarn into carrot. | | | |
| Make four more carrots for adult's hat, two more for children's. | | | |
| **ATTACHING CARROTS TO EARFLAPS** | | | |
| *For adult's hat only:* Using a 5' length of mc, insert crochet hook through st at top of carrot (not leaf), fold yarn in half, and place fold (midpoint) over hook end. | | | |
| With yarn doubled, make 25 chain sts (see illustration on page 55). Fasten off by pulling only one strand of yarn through loop on hook. Pull yarn ends tightly through top of hat and weave loose ends into bottom center of flap. | | | |
| Attach one carrot tassel to each flap. | | | |
| **ATTACHING CARROTS TO CROWN** | | | |
| Using a 3' length of mc, insert crochet hook through st at top of carrot (not leaf), fold yarn in half, and place fold (midpoint) over hook end. | | | |
| With yarn doubled, make 15 chain sts. | | | |

| | TODDLER | KID | ADULT M |
|---|---|---|---|
| Fasten off by pulling only one strand of yarn through loop on hook. Pull yarn ends tightly through top of hat and weave loose ends into inside. | | | |
| Join remaining carrots in the same manner. | | | |

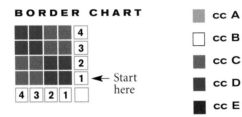

### BORDER CHART

4
3
2
1 ← Start here
4 3 2 1

- cc A
- cc B
- cc C
- cc D
- cc E

## Bobble for Bunny Tail

Each time you come to the square on the Bunny Chart marked "X," make a bobble for the bunny tail. Here's how:

**1.** Using cc B (white), (K1 in back loop, P1 in front loop, K1 in front loop, P1 in back loop) of same (first) st on left needle.

**2.** P4.

**3.** K4tog through the back loop.

**4.** Using left needle and cc E (brown), pick up and knit the closest cc E st; pass cc B (white) st over cc E st.

### BUNNY CHART

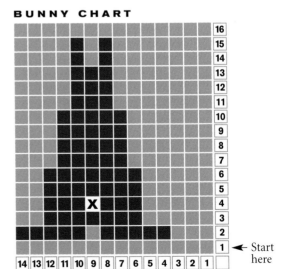

← Start here

## CARROT CHART

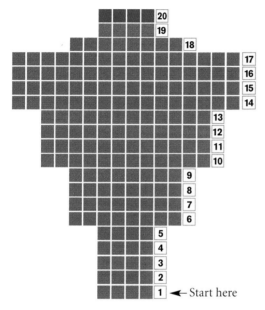

```
                    20
                    19
                       18
                          17
                          16
                          15
                          14
                    13
                    12
                    11
                    10
                  9
                  8
                  7
                  6
              5
              4
              3
              2
              1  ◄— Start here
```

**Detail of Leaf Loop**

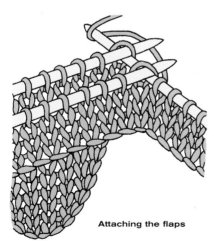

**Attaching the flaps**

## Chain Stitch

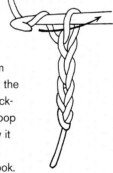

With one loop on your crochet hook, insert the hook under the working yarn from right to left. Twist the hook counter-clockwise to catch a loop of yarn, and draw it through the loop already on the hook.

# Morning Glories

Designed by Barbara Telford, Woodsmoke Woolworks

The color work in this hat is simpler than it looks, but if you haven't knitted with two strands of yarn before, practice before beginning. Many rows are worked in three colors (two carried, one knitted). The flower tassels are a great introduction to three-dimensional knitting. Some basic crocheting is also required. The hat pictured was knit with yarn listed at right; you may use any yarn that will provide the required gauge.

## Sizes and finished circumferences

Adult small, 19" (47.5cm); Adult medium, 20½" (51cm); Adult large, 22" (55cm)

**Yarn:** Briggs & Little Regal 100% wool

2 skeins mc (cream)

1 skein cc A (yellow)

1 skein cc B (green)

1 skein cc C (purple)

1 skein cc D (pink)

1 skein cc E (blue)

## Needles

One set #7 (4.5mm) dp needles *or size needed to obtain gauge*

## Gauge

20 sts = 4" (10cm) in St st, before blocking

## Other supplies

Stitch marker, #6 (4mm) crochet hook, yarn needle

---

**cc** = contrast color ◆ **cont** = continue ◆ **dp** = double pointed ◆ **inc** = increase ◆ **K** = knit **K2tog** = knit 2 stitches together ◆ **mc** = main color ◆ **P** = purl ◆ **psso** = pass slipped stitch over next stitch ◆ **rnd(s)** = round(s) ◆ **rs** = right side ◆ **sl** = slip ◆ **st(s)** = stitch(es) ◆ **St st** = stockinette stitch ◆ **ws** = wrong side

| KNITTING THE BAND | ADULT S | ADULT M | ADULT L |
|---|---|---|---|
| With mc, cast on | 96 sts | 104 sts | 112 sts |
| Place stitch marker on needle at end of first rnd. (Slip marker to end of each new rnd as completed, until hat is finished.) | | | |
| Knit | 12 rnds | 13 rnds | 13 rnds |
| **KNITTING THE PATTERN** | | | |
| Following the Trellis Chart on page 61, knit every row by reading each rnd from right to left, starting with line 1 at the bottom. Repeat the 8-st pattern to end of the rnd, then work line 2 to end of next rnd. Cont in this manner until the chart is finished. At the end of the chart, cut all yarns. | | | |
| With mc, knit | 4 rnds | 5 rnds | 5 rnds |
| **DECREASING FOR THE CROWN** | | | |
| Round 1: *K6, K2tog; repeat from * to end of rnd. You will have | 84 sts | 91 sts | 98 sts |
| Rounds 2, 4, 6, 8, 10, 12, and 14: Knit. | | | |
| Round 3: *K5, K2tog; repeat from * to end of rnd. You will have | 72 sts | 78 sts | 84 sts |
| Round 5: *K4, K2tog; repeat from * to end of rnd. You will have | 60 sts | 65 sts | 70 sts |
| Round 7: *K3, K2tog; repeat from * to end of rnd. You will have | 48 sts | 52 sts | 56 sts |
| Round 9: *K2, K2tog; repeat from * to end of rnd. You will have | 36 sts | 39 sts | 42 sts |
| Round 11: *K1, K2tog; repeat from * to end of rnd. You will have | 24 sts | 26 sts | 28 sts |
| Round 13: K2tog to end of rnd. You will have | 12 sts | 13 sts | 14 sts |
| **FINISHING THE HAT** | | | |
| Cut yarn. Using yarn needle, thread yarn end through sts on needle. Pull end through hole to ws. Flip hat inside out and weave in loose ends. | | | |

| KNITTING THE FLOWERS *(Make three)* | ADULT S | ADULT M | ADULT L |
|---|---|---|---|
| With two dp needles and cc B (green), cast on 4 sts, leaving 10" (25cm) of yarn end. Knit flowers in St st, knitting on odd rows, turning, and purling on even rows. | | | |
| Rows 1 and 3: Knit. | | | |
| Rows 2, 4, 6, 8, 10, 12, and 14: Purl. | | | |
| Row 5: Using cc C (purple), cc D (pink), or cc E (blue), inc 1 st in each st. (See pages 10–11 for guidance on making a 1-st inc in a st.) You will have | 8 sts | 8 sts | 8 sts |
| Row 7: Knit. | | | |
| Row 9: Inc 1 st in each st. You will have | 16 sts | 16 sts | 16 sts |
| Rows 11 and 13: Knit. | | | |
| Row 15: Inc 1 st in each st. You will have | 32 sts | 32 sts | 32 sts |
| Row 16: Knit. | | | |
| Row 17: Cast off in knit. Cut yarn, leaving end long enough to make a seam. | | | |
| With the rs (knit) inside, fold the flower vertically. Sew the long vertical edges together and turn the finished flower rs out. | | | |
| To make the flower stamen, use crochet hook and cc A (yellow) to chain st. (See page 55 for chain st instructions.) | 20 sts | 20 sts | 20 sts |
| To make the stem, fold in half a 3' (0.9m) strand of cc B (green). Insert crochet hook through a chain st halfway along one of the crocheted stamens. | | | |

| | ADULT S | ADULT M | ADULT L |
|---|---|---|---|
| Place folded end of cc B strand on end of hook and pull it through chain st. Don't pull through more than the fold. The cc B loop on the hook replaces the slipknot that usually starts a length of chain sts. | | | |
| With doubled cc B yarn handled as one strand, chain st | 15 sts | 15 sts | 15 sts |
| Pull joined stem and stamen through flower, from top to bottom, so fold in stamen is at base of flower. With cc B yarn end, sew across bottom of flower. When seaming, sew through chains to secure stem and stamen. | | | |
| Make two more flowers in remaining cc colors. | | | |
| **KNITTING THE LEAVES** *(Make three)* | | | |
| To make a leaf, use two dp needles and cc B (green); cast on | 3 sts | 3 sts | 3 sts |
| Row 1: K1, inc 2 in next st, K1. You will have | 5 sts | 5 sts | 5 sts |
| Row 2: P1, inc 1 in next st, P1, inc 1 in next st, P1. You will have | 7 sts | 7 sts | 7 sts |
| Row 3: K1, inc 1 in next st, K3, inc 1 in next st, K1. You will have | 9 sts | 9 sts | 9 sts |
| Row 4: P1, inc 1 in next st, P5, inc 1 in next st, P1. You will have | 11 sts | 11 sts | 11 sts |
| Row 5: Knit. | | | |
| Row 6: Purl. | | | |
| Row 7: K2tog, K7, K2tog. You will have | 9 sts | 9 sts | 9 sts |
| Rows 8, 10, 12, and 14: Purl. | | | |
| Row 9: K2tog, K5, K2tog. You will have | 7 sts | 7 sts | 7 sts |
| Row 11: K2tog, K3, K2tog. You will have | 5 sts | 5 sts | 5 sts |
| Row 13: K2tog, K1, K2tog. You will have | 3 sts | 3 sts | 3 sts |

| | ADULT S | ADULT M | ADULT L |
|---|---|---|---|
| Row 15: Sl1, K2tog, psso. You will have | 1 st | 1 st | 1 st |
| Cut yarn. Pull yarn end through st on needle. Sew to midpoint of stem and weave in all yarn ends inside work. | | | |
| Make two more leaves for the tassel. | | | |
| Attach flowers and leaves to top of hat by pulling ends through top hole. Tie a square knot and weave in loose ends. | | | |

## TRELLIS CHART

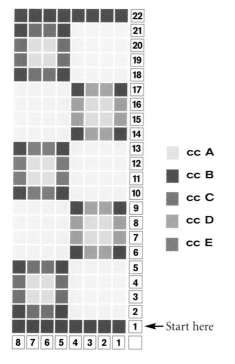

← Start here

cc A
cc B
cc C
cc D
cc E

## Color by Numbers

Carrying yarn across the back of a work can be challenging. Most rows in this pattern call for three colors, which means you knit one color and carry the other two across the wrong side until they are needed. Twist the active and carried strands when a float (the unused strand on the wrong side of the work) spans five stitches. Be sure to let the floats stay loose so that they don't pucker the fabric. When a color isn't used in a row, don't carry it across the back. Instead, let it float vertically, up to the next row where it will be used.

# Handpaint Hat

Designed by Linda Daniels, Northampton Wools

This pattern is easy and fun, and the finished project is warm and woolly. The hat was designed for a hand-painted yarn from Colinette Yarns called "Point Five" (we show it in two colors; see facing page and page 64), but other bulky yarns may be substituted. The knit is quite stretchy, so you may not need to add stitches to fit an average adult's head circumference. The multicolored yarn and contrasting brim and crown create a more complex design, but you can use all multicolor yarn or a single color. This hat knits up fast; you may find yourself making two, or three, or . . .

**Level:** Easy!

**Size and finished circumference**

Adult small–medium, 20" (51cm)

**Yarn**

1 skein mc (multi) Colinette Point Five
100% wool

1 skein cc (purple) bulky-weight wool

**Needles**

One set #13 (9mm) dp needles *or size needed
to obtain gauge*

**Gauge**

10 sts = 4" (10cm) in St st, before blocking

**Other supplies**

Stitch marker, yarn needle

---

**cc** = contrast color ◆ **dp** = double pointed
**K** = knit ◆ **K2tog** = knit 2 stitches together
**mc** = main color ◆ **rnd(s)** = round(s)
**st(s)** = stitch(es) ◆ **St st** = stockinette stitch

## KNITTING RIM AND HAT

With cc, loosely cast on 50 sts.

Join rnd, being careful not to twist sts. Place stitch marker at end of rnd. (Slip marker to end of each new rnd as completed.)

Rounds 1–5: Knit. Cut yarn.

Round 6: Change to mc and knit.

Round 7: Purl.

Round 8: Knit.

Round 9: Purl.

Rounds 10–18: Knit.

Rounds 19–22: Purl.

Rounds 23 and 24: Knit. Cut yarn; don't cast off.

## DECREASING FOR CROWN

Round 1: Change to cc, knit.

Round 2: *K8, K2tog; repeat from * to end of rnd. You will have 45 sts.

Round 3: *K7, K2tog; repeat from * to end of rnd. You will have 40 sts.

Round 4: *K6, K2tog; repeat from * to end of rnd. You will have 35 sts.

Round 5: *K5, K2tog; repeat from * to end of rnd. You will have 30 sts.

Round 6: *K4, K2tog; repeat from * to end of rnd. You will have 25 sts.

Round 7: *K3, K2tog; repeat from * to end of rnd. You will have 20 sts.

Round 8: K2, K2tog; repeat from * to end of rnd. You will have 15 sts.

Round 9: K2tog to last st, K1. You will have 8 sts.

## FINISHING THE HAT

Cut yarn. Thread end on yarn needle and pull through remaining sts. Weave in loose ends on inside of hat.

## Textured Yarns

If you've never knitted with textured yarn, don't expect to create a very smooth fabric — the knitted work is supposed to be nubby. The bigger your needles, the more the texture of the yarn shows.

# Double-Knit Headband

Designed by Nancy Lindberg

Double-knit fabric has two layers of fabric — and you knit both layers at the same time. This project teaches some new techniques and stitches, and there's a real thrill to seeing the double-knitted fabric grow. Once you've tried the lesser-known long-tail cast-on method, you'll be a fan. The kitchener stitch (a method for grafting together fabric edges) makes a seam invisible. The hat pictured was knit with yarns listed at right; you may use any yarn that will provide the required gauge.

## Sizes and finished circumferences

Child, 18½" (47cm); Adult medium, 20" (51cm); Adult large, 21½" (54.5cm)

**NOTE:** Don't let the finished circumference of the headband fool you. It will fit, even if your head is several inches larger, because double-knit fabric is very stretchy.

**Yarn:** Brown Sheep Nature Spun sport-weight 100% wool

**Child:** 1 skein mc (nervous green) and 1 skein cc (sunburst gold)

**Adult M:** 1 skein mc (cranberry fog) and 1 skein cc (sunburst gold)

**Adult L:** 1 skein mc (mountain purple) and 1 skein cc (sunburst gold)

## Needles

Two sets #5 (3.75mm) circular needles 16" (40cm) long *or size needed to obtain gauge*

## Gauge

18 sts = 4" (10cm) in double-knit st, measured on one side before blocking

## Other supplies

Stitch marker, yarn needle

---

**cc** = contrast color ◆ **K** = knit ◆ **mc** = main color ◆ **P** = purl
**rnd(s)** = round(s) ◆ **sl** = slip ◆ **st(s)** = stitch(es)

| KNITTING THE HEM | CHILD | ADULT M | ADULT L |
|---|---|---|---|
| Using long-tail cast-on method (see pages 8–9), one circular needle, and cc, cast on | 84 sts | 90 sts | 98 sts |
| Place stitch marker at beginning of sts. Join rnd, being careful not to twist sts. (Slip marker to end of each new rnd as completed.) | | | |
| Rounds 1 and 2: Knit. Don't cut yarn. | | | |
| Rounds 3–5: With mc, knit. Don't cut yarn. | | | |
| Unravel the cast-on rnd st by st, placing live sts on second needle (see "Double Knitting" on the facing page). | | | |
| With original needle and purl sides together, join layers as follows: *Move both yarns to back, K1 from front needle with mc, move both yarns to front, P1 from back needle with cc; repeat from * to end of rnd. All sts are on the original needle. (See "Double Knitting" on the facing page.) | | | |
| You will have | 168 sts | 180 sts | 196 sts |
| KNITTING THE PATTERN | | | |
| Knit the pattern, using the double-knit method and following one of the two charts for your size (see page 71). Read each rnd from right to left, starting with line 1 at the bottom. | | | |
| SEPARATING THE LAYERS | | | |
| Round 1 (front needle): *With yarn to back, K1 with mc, sl purl st on spare circular needle; repeat from * to end of rnd. | | | |
| Sts on front needle | 84 | 90 | 98 |
| Sts on back needle | 84 | 90 | 98 |
| Rounds 2–4 (front needle): With mc and ignoring sts on back needle, knit sts on front needle. | | | |

# Double Knitting

## Step 1:

After knitting five rounds, unravel the cast-on round stitch by stitch; place stitches on a spare circular needle.

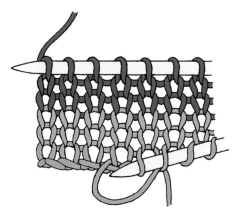

Unraveling cast-on stitches: Step 1

## Step 2:

With the five rounds of knitting folded wrong sides together, join layers by alternating a knit stitch from the front needle and a purl stitch from the back needle. As you work, think of each stitch as really a pair of stitches (one knit stitch and one purl stitch). With both yarns in back, knit front stitch with mc. Move both yarns to front, purl back stitch with cc.

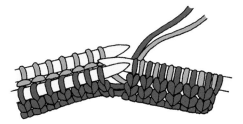

Joining layers to form double knitting: Step 2

| | CHILD | ADULT M | ADULT L |
|---|---|---|---|
| **NOTE:** The second side (back needle) has one less row. This is intentional. Once you have joined the sides with the kitchener stitch, they will match perfectly. Cut yarn. | | | |
| Rounds 1–3 (back needle): Turn headband inside out so right (knit) side is facing you. With cc and ignoring needle holding longer fabric, knit to end of rnd. | | | |
| **FINISHING THE HAT** | | | |
| When the second side is complete, cut the yarn, leaving a long length of cc. | | | |
| Kitchener-stitch the layers together (see page 70 for instructions). | | | |

# Kitchener Stitch

**1.** Hold two fabric layers together with purl sides inside. Using a needle, draw yarn through first stitch of front needle as if to knit; slip stitch off.

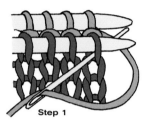

Step 1

**2.** Draw yarn through second stitch of front needle as if to purl; leave stitch on needle.

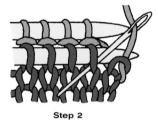

Step 2

**3.** Draw yarn through first stitch of back needle as if to purl; slip stitch off.

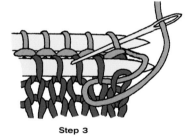

Step 3

**4.** Draw yarn through second stitch of back needle as if to knit; leave stitch on. Repeat steps until no stitches remain on needles.

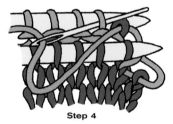

Step 4

# How to Use Double-Knit Charts

In the charts at right, each square represents a pair of stiches: 1 knit and 1 purl.

**mc** ▮ With both yarns in back, knit stitch with mc. Move both yarns to front, and purl stitch with cc.

**cc** ☒ With both yarns in back, knit stitch with cc. Move both yarns to front and purl stitch with mc.

# Double-Knit Headband Charts

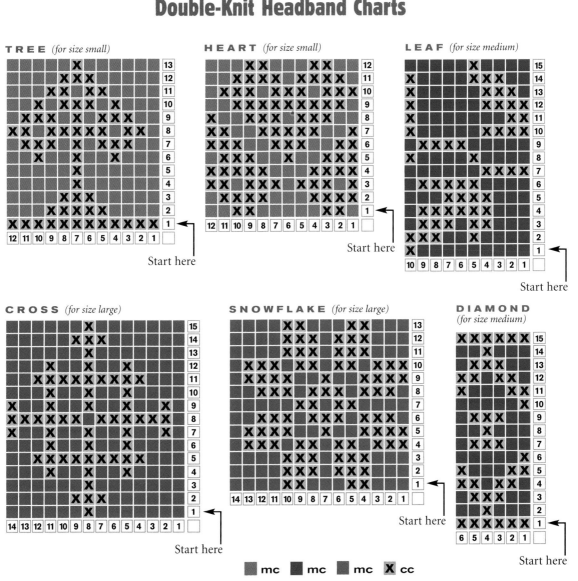

**TREE** *(for size small)*

Start here

**HEART** *(for size small)*

Start here

**LEAF** *(for size medium)*

Start here

**CROSS** *(for size large)*

Start here

**SNOWFLAKE** *(for size large)*

Start here

**DIAMOND** *(for size medium)*

Start here

mc   mc   mc   **X** cc

# Needle-Felted Hat

Designed by Nancy Lindberg

Soft, bulky, fuzzy . . . anything goes when knitting this hat. Try using yarn from your latest project or experiment with a new yarn. A soft dense knit is desirable — the stiffer the yarn, the scratchier the hat. The hat pictured was knit with yarns listed at right; you may use any yarn that will provide the required gauge. In this pattern, the cuff turns under to the inside of the hat for an attractive hem, and an easy felting technique completes the design. There are row-by-row instructions for two sizes.

**Level:** Easy!

**Sizes and finished circumferences**

Adult small, 18" (45cm); Adult medium, 20" (50cm)

**Yarn:** Galway worsted-weight 100% wool and
Persian crewel yarn 100% wool

    **Adult S:** 1 skein mc (royal blue)
    1 skein cc (yellow) crewel yarn
    1 skein cc (orange) crewel yarn
    1 skein cc (green) crewel yarn

    **Adult M:** 1 skein mc (royal blue)
    1 skein cc (yellow) crewel yarn
    1 skein cc (orange) crewel yarn
    1 skein cc (green) crewel yarn

**Needles**

One #8 (5mm) circular needle, 16" (40cm) long,
*or size needed to obtain gauge*

One #7 (4.5mm) circular needle, 16" (40cm) long,
*or one size smaller than larger circular needle*

One set #8 (5mm) dp needles *or same size as
larger circular needle*

**Gauge**

20 sts = 4" in St st on larger needles, before blocking

**Other supplies**

Four stitch markers, yarn needle

---

**cc** = contrast color ◆ **dp** = double pointed ◆ **K** = knit ◆ **K2tog** = knit 2 stitches together
**K3tog** = knit 3 stitches together ◆ **mc** = main color ◆ **M1** = make 1 ◆ **rnd(s)** = round(s)
**ssk** = slip, slip, knit 2 stitches together ◆ **st(s)** = stitch(es) ◆ **St st** = Stockinette stitch

| KNITTING THE CUFF | ADULT S | ADULT M |
|---|---|---|
| With mc and smaller circular needle, cast on | 86 sts | 90 sts |
| Place stitch marker. Join rnd, being careful not to twist sts. (Slip marker to end of each new rnd as completed.) | | |
| Knit every rnd until cuff length is | 3" | 3" |
| **KNITTING THE HAT** | | |
| Round 1: Repeat from * (see column at right) to end of rnd. | *K8, M1, K9, M1; K1 | *K9, M1 |
| You will have | 96 sts | 100 sts |
| Round 2: With larger circular needle, purl to end of rnd. | | |
| Knit rnds until length from purl rnd is | 5" | 6" |
| **DECREASING FOR THE CROWN** | | |
| Round 1: Knit 1 rnd, placing a marker after the following sts | 24, 48, 72, 96 | 25, 50, 75, 100 |
| Round 2: *Knit to 2 sts before marker, K2tog, slip marker, K1, ssk; repeat from * to end of rnd. You will have | 88 sts | 92 sts |
| Round 3: Knit to end of rnd. | | |
| Repeat Rounds 2 and 3 until you have | 8 sts | 12 sts |
| It will become increasingly difficult to knit on circular needles as the sts are reduced. Transfer the sts to dp needles when the circular is too long. | | |
| **ADDING THE TOP KNOT** | | |
| Round 1: Repeat from * (see column at right) to end of rnd. You will have | *K2tog | *K3tog |
| Round 2: With two dp needles, start I-cord. (See page 16 for complete instructions.) | 4 sts | 4 sts |

| | ADULT S | ADULT M |
|---|---|---|
| Knit I-cord until length is | 3" | 3" |
| Cut yarn. Thread end on yarn needle, draw yarn through sts,and fasten end to hat, creating a loop. | | |
| **NEEDLE FELTING AND FINISHING THE HAT** | | |
| Using ccs, apply needle felting as described in box below. | | |
| Fold cast-on edge of hat cuff to inside of hat and sew in place using an overhand stitch. | | |

# Needle Felting

No embroidery or other special skills are required for the free-flowing decoration on this hat. All you need is a felting needle (available at fiber art supply stores), a 3-inch-thick foam block (a thick sponge works well), and several yard-long pieces of 100% wool yarn. Here's how it works.

If you were to look at a piece of wool yarn under a microscope, you would see that it's composed of many fine fibers. When you lay a strand of yarn on knitted wool fabric and plunge a felting needle through the yarn and fabric, the tiny barbs on the needle catch the fibers of the wool and interlock them – sort of like Velcro.

Before applying the felting to the hat, experiment on a knitted swatch. Place the swatch flat on the foam piece. Lay a strand of yarn on the fabric in any pattern you wish, and then attach the yarn to the fabric by plunging the needle straight down through both. Keep the needle perpendicular to the surface as you repeatedly stab the fabric with an up-and-down motion. Move along the yarn until the entire piece is attached to the fabric.

**Tip:** Tack the strands into position at 1-inch intervals along the length of the yarn, then go back and work over every bit of the yarn with the needle until it is firmly attached to the knitted fabric.

# Felted Sherpa Hat

Designed by Cynthia Walker, Stony Hill Fiberarts

The magical transformation from wool to felt is an ancient art. When wool fibers are combined with hot water, soap, and moving pressure, they bind together, creating a firm, felted fabric that is durable, permanently shaped, and warm even when wet. The hat pictured was knit with yarn listed at right; you may use any yarn that will provide the required gauge.

---

**dp** = double pointed ◆ **K** = knit ◆ **K2tog** = knit 2 stitches together ◆ **inc** = increase **Inc1** = increase 1 ◆ **rnd(s)** = round(s) **rs** = right side ◆ **st(s)** = stitch(es) ◆ **ws** = wrong side

---

**Size**

Baby/toddler

**Finished circumference**

16" (40.5cm); use double-knit or sport-weight yarn for a smaller circumference

> NOTE: The finished circumference is approximate. The yarn and the point at which you stop felting will determine the size. For instructions on making a hat with a larger circumference, see "Bigger and Better" on page 79; for information on other yarns suitable for felting, see "Felting Tips" on page 84.

**Yarn:** Henry's Attic 'Texas,' 55% mohair/ 45% wool, hand-dyed by the designer

1 skein (80 yds) white or beige/sage/blue

**Needles**

One #10½ (6.5mm) circular needle, 16" (40cm) long, *or size needed to obtain gauge*

One set #10½ (6.5mm) dp needles *or same size as circular needle*

**Gauge**

12–16 sts = 4" (10cm) in garter st, before felting

**Other supplies**

Two stitch markers, yarn needle, laundry detergent, bowl to match head size

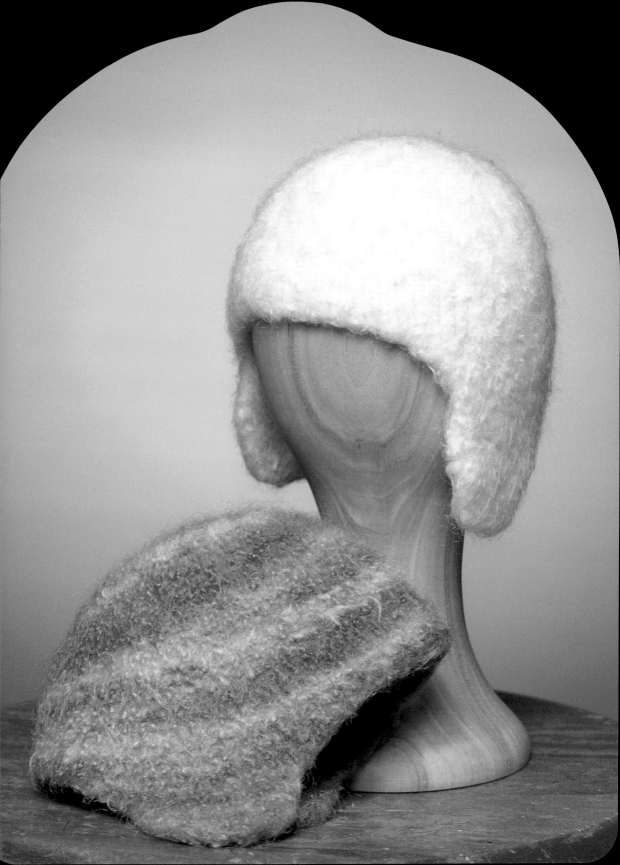

## KNITTING FIRST EARFLAP

**NOTE:** Incs in this hat are made by knitting into the front *and* back of the next st. Work earflaps on circular needle, but turn at end of sts so you knit straight rows of garter st. Place marker to the right of both flaps as they're worked; inc rows are made with the rs facing you.

With #10½ (6.5mm) circular needle, cast on 5 sts.

Row 1: Knit to end of row.

Row 2: K1, Inc1, K1, Inc1, K1, place marker on side of fabric facing you. You'll have 7 sts.

Row 3: Knit to end of row.

Row 4: K1, Inc1, K3, Inc1, K1. You'll have 9 sts.

Row 5: Knit to end of row.

Row 6: K1, Inc1, K5, Inc1, K1. You'll have 11 sts.

Row 7: Knit to end of row.

Row 8: K1, Inc1, K7, Inc1, K1. You'll have 13 sts.

Rows 9–17: Knit to end of each row.

Row 18: K1, Inc1, K9, inc1, K1. You'll have 15 sts.

Row 19: Knit to end of row.

Row 20: K1, Inc1, K1, Inc1, K7, Inc1, K1, Inc1, K1. You'll have 19 sts.

Row 21: Knit to end of row.

Row 22: K1, Inc1, K15, Inc1, K1. You'll have 21 sts and 11 ridges lengthwise. Cut yarn.

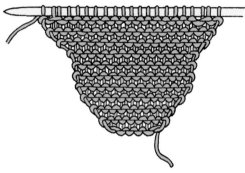

Knitting the earflap

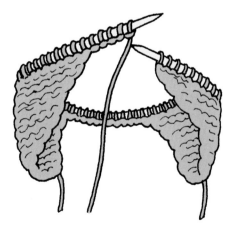

Joining the earflaps

## KNITTING SECOND EARFLAP

Turn the first earflap so the ws is facing you; push it to the bottom of needle and make the second flap on the same needle without removing the first.

With new yarn, cast on 5 sts.

Follow Knitting First Earflap Rows 1–22. Do not cut yarn at end of second flap. Instead, turn the work to start a new row.

## JOINING THE EARFLAPS

Join earflaps by casting on sts. The back of the hat will have 5 sts between flaps, and the front of the hat will have 13 sts between flaps.

Round 1: Knit to end of row of second earflap, cast on 13 sts, scoot first earflap up and knit to end of row, cast on 5 sts. You'll have 60 sts.

Round 2: Join rnd being careful not to twist stitches. K21 (first earflap), then slip a stitch marker onto the needle. One flap is a row shorter, but don't worry about it. When the hat is felted, the flaps will look identical.

## KNITTING THE SIDES

The stitch marker indicates the start of a new round. Knit in rnd until 6" or 7" (15cm or 17.5cm) from where you joined the rnd.

## DECREASING FOR CROWN

Round 1: Slip marker to start of rnd, *K4, K2tog; repeat from * to end of rnd. You'll have 50 sts.

Round 2: Knit.

# Bigger and Better

If you want a larger hat, increase the number of stitches you cast on between the flaps. Keep the same distance *ratios* between flaps: The distance between the flaps at the back of the head is about 40 percent of that at the front of the head. If you're increasing the circumference, you'll probably have to also increase the depth. To do this, knit more rows. Felting decreases the finished size by approximately 25 to 30 percent.

| |
|---|
| Round 3: *K3, K2tog; repeat from * to end of rnd. You'll have 40 sts. Switch to dp needles when sts are too stretched on circular needle. |
| Round 4: Knit. |
| Round 5: *K2, K2tog; repeat from * to end of rnd. You'll have 30 sts. |
| Round 6: Knit. |
| Round 7: *K1, K2tog; repeat from * to end of rnd. You'll have 20 sts. |
| Round 8: Knit. |
| Round 9: *K2tog; repeat from * to end of rnd. You'll have 10 sts. |
| Round 10: *K2tog; repeat from * to end of rnd. You'll have 5 sts. |
| Cut yarn. Thread end on yarn needle and pull through remaining sts. Weave in loose ends on ws of work. What you have looks like a ridiculously big and baggy hat, but just watch what happens during the felting process! Follow the directions for felting in the box at the right. |

◁ When you knit a hat that will be shrunk by felting, the piece is a loose knit on large needles and is much larger than the finished, felted hat. Your work may look a bit odd, as you can see in the photo at left. But take heart — the felting process will transform it!

## Cynthia's Felting Technique

**1.** Set washing machine on lowest water level, fill with hot water, and put a small amount of laundry detergent in the machine.

**2.** Agitate. The amount of time needed for felting the hat may vary. Check often to ensure that the hat doesn't felt too much and to find any holes that may appear where you wove in a loose end. If you find a hole early enough, simply mend it with extra yarn and throw the hat back into the washer to agitate longer.

**3.** When the hat is felted as desired, rinse it in cold water, shape it a bit, and then stretch it over a bowl that is the same size as the head it will fit. Let the hat dry for a couple of days. Trim off any excess fuzz.

**4.** To care for the finished hat, wash it in lukewarm water, rinse, reshape, and air-dry.

**5.** With a front-loading washer, you'll have to let it go through an entire cycle. It may need a few agitation cycles to felt it to your liking.

# Adult's Felt Hat

Designed by Bev Galeskas, Fiber Trends

Knit with doubled yarn, this project is great for those who have mastered basic stitches and are ready for the next step. This pattern takes the guesswork out of creating a felted hat to fit your head because you mount the felted hat on a bowl to air-dry. The decrease at the crown is very attractive after felting. Remember: Knitting must be loose to felt properly. The hat pictured was knit with yarn listed at right; you may use any yarn that will provide the required gauge.

**dp** = double pointed ◆ **K** = knit ◆ **K2tog** = knit 2 stitches together ◆ **M1** = make 1 **rnd(s)** = round(s) ◆ **ssk** = slip, slip, knit **st(s)** = stitch(es) ◆ **St st** = stockinette stitch

### Size

Adult small–large

### Finished circumference

The finished size is controlled by the size of the bowl you use to block the felted hat. Choose a bowl that is slightly larger than the desired head circumference. (If you can't measure the wearer's head, see page 8 for average sizes.)

### Yarn

2 skeins forest floor Brown Sheep Handpaint Originals 70% mohair/30% wool

1 skein enchanted forest Brown Sheep Nature Spun 100% wool

**NOTE:** The hat is knit with with one strand of Handpaint Originals and one strand of Nature Spun. The two yarns are held together and handled as a single yarn. For information on other yarns for felting, see "Felting Tips" on page 84.

### Needles

One #11 (8mm) circular needle, 24" (60cm) or 29" (73.5cm) long, *or size needed to obtain gauge*

One set #11 (8mm) dp needles *or same size as circular needle*

### Gauge

10–12 sts = 4" (10cm) in St st, before felting

### Other supplies

Stitch marker, yarn needle, zippered pillow protector, laundry detergent, bowl, hairbrush (or pet-grooming slicker for mohair)

## KNITTING THE BRIM

With #11 (8mm) circular needle, cast on 70 sts with one strand of each yarn held together. Join rnd, being careful not to twist sts. Place stitch marker at end of rnd. (Slip marker to end of each new rnd as completed.)

Rounds 1–4: Knit.

Round 5: *K8, M1; repeat from * to end of rnd. You will have 80 sts.

Rounds 6–9: Knit.

Round 10: *K8, M1; repeat from * to end of rnd. You will have 90 sts.

Rounds 11–14: Knit.

## BEGINNING THE CROWN

Round 1: *(K2tog) 4 times, K1; repeat from * to end of rnd. You will have 50 sts.

Rounds 2 and 3: Knit.

Round 4: *K2, M1, K3, M1; repeat from * to end of rnd. You will have 70 sts.

Continue knitting in rnds of St st until 7" (18cm) from beginning of crown.

## Felting Tips

Any animal fiber, such as wool, alpaca, and mohair, will felt, as long as it hasn't been treated. Washable wool, bleached white wool, super-wash wool, cotton, rayon, silk, and synthetic fibers don't felt. Many off-white and light colors do not felt well, if at all. It's fun trying various fibers, but the yarn must shrink when it is washed.

Some yarns felt much faster and may also become smaller than others. Some may not felt to an attractive fabric. Always knit a swatch in stockinette stitch and felt it to test your yarn. Note the measurements before and after the process so you won't be disappointed if your hat shrinks too much. And remember: Knitting must be loose to felt properly.

## DECREASING FOR CROWN

Change to dp needles when work is too short for circular needles.

Round 1: *K5, K2tog; repeat from * to end of rnd. You will have 60 sts.

Rounds 2, 3, 5, 6, 8, 10, and 12: Knit.

Round 4: *K4, ssk; repeat from * to end of rnd. You will have 50 sts.

Round 7: *K3, K2tog; repeat from * to end of rnd. You will have 40 sts.

Round 9: *K2, ssk; repeat from * to end of rnd. You will have 30 sts.

Round 11: *K1, K2tog; repeat from * to end of rnd. You will have 20 sts.

Round 13: *Ssk; repeat from * to end of rnd. You will have 10 sts.

Round 14: *K2tog to end of rnd. You will have 5 sts.

## FINISHING THE HAT

Cut yarn. Thread the end through a yarn needle and pull through the remaining 5 sts. Tighten. Weave in yarn ends on wrong side (inside) of work.

## Bev's Easy Felting

1. Place hat in a zippered pillow protector to protect your washer from excess lint washed out during felting.

2. Adjust washer setting for hot wash, low water level, and longest cycle. Add a little laundry detergent and start the machine.

3. For more control over the felting process, don't use the washer's rinse and spin cycles. It's hard to predict the amount of shrinkage that will occur during agitation and rinsing, and, occasionally, the spin cycle sets a permanent crease in felted fabric. During agitation, check the progress every 5 minutes. Set the washer to agitate longer, if needed. When the hat seems to be the right size, remove it and thoroughly hand rinse. Blot with towels to remove as much water as possible, then check the fit. If necessary, return the hat to the washer for more felting.

4. While it's still wet, stretch the finished hat over a bowl slightly larger than the head size. Leave the hat on the form until it is completely dry.

5. Brush hat to remove wool clumps.

6. To tweak a hat's shape, apply steam.

# Child's Felt Hat

Designed by Bev Galeskas, Fiber Trends

The rolled edge around the crown may appear to be sewn, but it is made with a spare needle and a simple K2tog. The turned-back brim is shaped with short rows and is wider in the front. This is a great project if you want to learn how to make short rows. For panache, tie a ribbon around the brim. The hat pictured was knit with yarn listed at right; you may use any yarn that will provide the required gauge.

**dp** = double pointed ◆ **K** = knit
**K2tog** = knit 2 stitches together ◆ **M1** = make 1 ◆ **P** = purl ◆ **rnd(s)** = round(s)
**rs** = right side ◆ **ssk** = slip, slip, knit
**st(s)** = stitch(es) ◆ **St st** = stockinette stitch ◆ **W&T** = wrap and turn (see box on page 88) ◆ **ws** = wrong side

## Size
Personalized fit

## Finished circumference
Up to 21½". The exact finished size is controlled by the size of the bowl you use to block the felted hat. Choose a bowl that is slightly larger than the desired head circumference. (If you cannot measure the head size of the person who will be wearing this hat, see page 8 for average head sizes.)

## Yarn
1 skein periwinkle Brown Sheep Lamb's Pride worsted 85% wool/15% mohair
**NOTE:** For information about other suitable yarns for felting, see "Felting Tips" on page 84.

## Needles
One #10½ (7mm) circular needle, 16" (40cm) long, *or size needed to obtain gauge*
One set 10½ (7mm) dp needles *or same size as circular needle*
One spare circular needle, 24" (60cm) long, several sizes smaller than circular needle

## Gauge
14 sts = 4" (10cm) in St st, before felting

## Other supplies
Bowl slightly larger than head circumference, hairbrush (or pet-grooming slicker for mohair), laundry detergent, stitch ring marker, tapestry needle

# How to Wrap and Turn

Turning work before the end of a row and working back along the row is a great way to increase depth, but you can end up with a small hole. The wrap and turn (W&T) method solves this problem.

## On Knit Rows:

**1.** Work up to the turning point; slip next stitch (purlwise) onto the right needle.

**2.** Move the yarn between the needles to the front of the work; return slipped stitch to the left needle.

**3.** Move the yarn between the needles back; turn to work in other direction. (W&T is complete.)

## On Purl Rows:

**1.** Work up to the turning point; slip next stitch (purlwise) onto the right needle.

**2.** Move the yarn between the needles to the back of the work; return slipped stitch to the left needle.

**3.** Move the yarn between the needles forward; turn to work in other direction. (W&T is complete.)

## Knitting W&T stitches

When you come to the wrapped stitches, knit them together with the stitch they wrap. Insert the right needle into wrap, then into stitch, and knit the two together.

Using #10½ circular needle, cast on 77 sts. **NOTE:** Do not join. Brim is worked back and forth in rows of garter st.

Row 1: Purl; turn.

Row 2: (K4, M1) 9 times, K2, M1, K1, M1, K2, (M1, K4) 8 times, M1, K2, W&T. There will be 2 unworked sts on left needle. You will have a total of 97 sts (worked and unworked) on needles.

Row 3: P93, W&T. There will be 2 unworked sts on left needle.

**NOTE:** For Rows 4–15 you are knitting 1 less st before each W&T.

Row 4: K92, W&T.

Row 5: P91, W&T.

Row 6: K90, W&T.

Row 7: P89, W&T.

Row 8: K88, W&T.

Row 9: P87, W&T.

Row 10: K86, W&T.

Row 11: P85, W&T.

Row 12: K84, W&T.

Row 13: P83, W&T.

Row 14: K82, W&T.

Row 15: P81, W&T.

Row 16: K7, (K2tog, K7) 3 times, K2tog, K9, (K2tog, K7) 3 times, K2tog, K5, W&T. There will be 2 unworked sts before previous W&T on left needle. You will have a total of 89 sts (worked and unworked) on needles.

**NOTE:** For Rows 17–21 you are knitting 2 less sts before each W&T.

Row 17: P69, W&T.

Row 18: K67, W&T.

Row 19: P65, W&T.

Row 20: K63, W&T.

Row 21: P61, W&T.

Row 22: Knit to end of row. Do not turn. You will have 89 sts on needles.

## Hide and Seek

When you're ready to knit a full row, hide the yarn wrap on select stitches. Insert the right needle into the wrap, then into the stitch on the left needle. Knit the two loops as one to create one stitch.

## BEGINNING THE CROWN

Bring opposite end of knitting up to point of left needle. Place marker onto right needle to mark beginning of rnd. (Slip marker at end of each new rnd as completed.) Join by beginning Round 1, being careful not to twist sts.

Round 1: Knit, working remaining wraps into new sts.

Round 2: *K2tog, K1; repeat from * to last 2 sts, K2tog. You will have 59 sts.

Rounds 3 and 4: Knit.

Round 5: K1, M1, *K3, M1; repeat from * to last st, K1. You will have 79 sts.

Knit: 22 rnds.

Next Round: K1, *K39, M1; repeat from * to end of rnd. You will have 81 sts.

Knit 1 rnd.

Purl 5 rnds.

## FORMING THE BAND

With the spare smaller circular needle and ws facing you, pick up the back loops of the last knit rnd (6 rnds below needle) around the entire crown. You will have 81 loops on the spare needle.

With ws together (purl side out), fold the purl rnds so the two needles are together. Hold both needles in your left hand.

Next Round: With working needle and rs facing you, knit together 1 st from the front needle and 1 st from the back needle. Repeat around, forming a rolled band.

Knit 2 rnds.

## DECREASING FOR CROWN

Change to dp needles when you have fewer sts and working on a circular needle is difficult.

Round 1: *K7, K2tog; repeat from * to end of rnd. You will have 72 sts.

Rounds 2 and 3: Knit.

Round 4: *K6, ssk; repeat from * to end of rnd. You will have 63 sts.

Rounds 5 and 6: Knit.

Round 7: *K5, K2tog; repeat from * to end of rnd. You will have 54 sts.

Rounds 8 and 9: Knit.

Round 10: *K4, ssk; repeat from * to end of rnd. You will have 45 sts.

Round 11: Knit.

Round 12: *K3, K2tog; repeat from * to end of rnd. You will have 36 sts.

Round 13: Knit.

Round 14: *K2, ssk; repeat from * to end of rnd. You will have 27 sts.

Round 15: Knit.

Round 16: *K1, K2tog; repeat from * to end of rnd. You will have 18 sts.

Round 17: Knit.

Round 18: *Ssk; repeat from * to end of rnd. You will have 9 sts.

## FINISHING THE HAT

Cut yarn. With a tapestry needle, thread end through remaining sts and pull together tightly. Fasten off. Weave in all yarn ends.

Felt hat according to "Bev's Easy Felting" on page 85.

# Acknowledgments

**Many thanks to**

The knitters who helped make the projects for this book:
Pam Art, Ann Burch, Kathleen M. Case, Laurie Figary, and Alison Kolesar

The companies that supplied yarn:
Brown Sheep Company of Mitchell, Nebraska;
Classic Elite Yarns of Lowell, Massachusetts;
and Nordic Fiber Arts of Durham, New Hampshire

The yarn stores that offered invaluable advice:
The Naked Sheep of Bennington, Vermont;
Northampton Wools of Northampton, Massachusetts;
Webs of Northampton, Massachusetts;
and Woolcot & Co. of Cambridge, Massachusetts

# Contributing Designers

**Linda Daniels, Northampton Wools**

11 Pleasant Street
Northampton, MA 01060
(413) 586-4331
e-mail: NohoKnit@aol.com

Since 1988, **Linda Daniels** has owned and operated Northampton Wools, a full-service retail store offering knitting classes and a wide selection of yarns from around the world. *Interweave Knits* has featured many of her patterns, and she designed and knit actor Michael Caine's vest and several sweaters for the movie *The Cider House Rules.*

**Beverly Galeskas, Fiber Trends**

P.O. Box 7266
East Wenatchee, WA 98802
(509) 884-8631
www.fibertrends.com

**Beverly Galeskas** is the owner and founder of Fiber Trends Pattern Company. Along with other designing, Bev is always looking for new ways to use the fascinating technique of knitting and felting (fulling) to create unique garments, accessories, and toys. She has taught classes at TNNA, Stitches, and many other knitting and fiber shows. "I believe my experiences of learning to knit as an adult and then teaching beginning knitting in my yarn store were the best training for writing patterns for others," she says.

**Deb and Lynda Gemmell, Cabin Fever**

111 Nottawasaga Street
Orillia, ON L3V 3J7
Canada
(800) 671-9112
www.cabinfever.ca

Canadian sisters **Deb and Lynda Gemmell** own and operate Cabin Fever, which sells wool and knitting supplies. In addition to hats, the innovative duo designs dozens of patterns for sweaters, socks, and other apparel that are sold in yarn shops across North America. Most are knit in the round and in one piece, with virtually no sewing required. Plus sizes are also a standard element of most of their patterns.

**Melinda Goodfellow, Yankee Knitter Designs**

369 Tanner Marsh Road
P.O. Box 304
Guilford, CT 06437
(203) 453-2033

**Melinda Goodfellow** has been knitting since she was six years old. After designing sweater patterns for her mother's yarn store, she founded her own business, Yankee Knitter Designs, which features classic patterns and easy-to-follow instructions.

## Nancy Lindberg

69 East Golden Lake Road
Circle Pines, MN 55014
e-mail: Nlpatterns@prodigy.net

Nancy Lindberg developed her teaching skills while owning a yarn shop in Minneapolis for more than a decade. She moved on to pattern designing and continues to teach, which has garnered a large and faithful following. Her patterns appeal to all knitting levels and are available in yarn shops across the United States.

## Barbara Telford,
## Woodsmoke Woolworks

1335 Route 102
Upper Gagetown, NB E5M 1R5
Canada
(506) 488-2044
e-mail: woodsmke@nbnet.nb.ca

Barbara Telford doesn't remember not knowing how to knit. A member of the Canadian Knitwear Designers Association and a juried member of the New Brunswick Craft Council, she runs Woodsmoke Woolworks, a farm-based knitwear and design shop. "I don't know where the hats came from," she says, "but I am glad they came."

## Cindy Walker,
## Stony Hill Fiberarts

3525 Durham Road
Raleigh, NC 27614
(888) 849-9440
www.stonyhillfiberarts.com

Cindy Walker established Stony Hill Fiberarts in 1994. Her company produces felted baby hats, baby booties, and slippers; felted knitting patterns that are simply written; hand-dyed yarn to ensure reliable felting results; and whimsical, handcrafted knitting needles. Cindy says, "Knitting has been my saving grace. I firmly believe that when we engage ourselves in some type of art, we expand our life experience in such a positive way that all we come in contact with is enriched: ourselves, our families, our world. I am grateful to have discovered this truth. And . . . it's cheaper than therapy!"

# Index

*Note:* Page numbers for charts are in **bold;** those for photos and illustrations are in *italics.*

**A**bbreviations, 8
Adult's Felt Hat, 82–85, *83,* **84–85**
Adult's hat/head sizes, 8

**B**aby or fingering yarn, 5
Baby's hat/head size, 8
Bar increase, 10, *10*
Beret, Three-Guage, 40–43, *41, 42*
Binding off, 9, *9*
Blocking, 15, *15*
Bulky-weight yarn, 5
Bunnies and Carrots, 48–55, *49,* **50–55,** *55*

**C**arrot Top, 18–21, *19,* **20–21**
Casting on/off, 8–9, *9, 47*
Chain stitch (crochet), 55, *55*
Child's Felt Hat, 86–90, *87,* **88–90**
Child's hat/head size, 8
Chunky-weight yarn, 5
Circular needles, 5, 6, 14
Color Me Bright, 36–39, *37,* **38–39**
Color (multi) knitting, 4, 14–15, *15,* 61
Conversion chart for needles, **6**
Crochet chain stitch, 55, *55*
Crochet hooks, 6, 11, *11*

**D**aniels, Linda, 62, 92
Decreasing, 12, *12*
Double-knit (DK) yarn, 5
Double-Knit Headband, 66–71, *67,* **68–69,**
   *69–70,* **71**
Double knitting, 69, *69*

Double-pointed needles, 5, 6, *13,* 13–14, 15
Dropped stitches, picking up, 11, *11*
Dye lots of yarn, 5
Dyeing, Kool-Aid, 39

**F**ake fur effect, 85
Felted Sherpa Hat, 76–81, *77–78,* **78–79,** *80,* **81**
Felting tips, 75, 81, 84, 85
Fingering or baby yarn, 5
Finishing hats, 16–17, *16–17*
Fitting (sizing) hats, 8

**G**aleskas, Beverly, 82, 85, 86, 92
Gauge (tension), 7, *7*
Gemmell, Deb, 18, 36, 44, 92
Gemmell, Lynda, 32, 36, 92
Goodfellow, Melinda, 22, 92

**H**andpaint Hat, 62–65, *63, 64,* **65**
Headband, Double-Knit, 66–71, *67,* **68–69,**
   *69–70,* **71**
Head vs. hat size, 8

**I**-cords, *16,* 16–17
Increasing, 10–11, *10–11*
Itching, avoiding, 4

**J**oining new yarn, 13, *13*

**K**2tog (knit 2 stitches together), 8, 12, *12*
Kitchener stitch, 70, *70*

Knitting, 4–17
  abbreviations, 8
  binding off, 9, *9*
  blocking, 15, *15*
  casting on/off, 8–9, *9, 47*
  circular needles, 5, 6, 14
  color (multi) knitting, 4, 14–15, *15*, 61
  decreasing, 12, *12*
  double knitting, 69, *69*
  double-pointed needles, 5, 6, *13*, 13–14, 15
  dropped stitches, picking up, 11, *11*
  finishing hats, 16–17, *16–17*
  fitting (sizing) hats, 8
  gauge (tension), 7, *7*
  increasing, 10–11, *10–11*
  joining new yarn, 13, *13*
  needles, 5–6, **6**
  seams, sewing, 16, *16*
  yarn, 4–5
Knitting bag, contents of, 6
Knitting in the round, 6, 13–14, *13–14*
Kool-Aid dyeing, 39

Lindberg, Nancy, 26, 40, 66, 72, 93
Long-tail cast on, 8–9, *9*

Make 1 with left/right slant, 10–11, *10–11*
Markers, 14
Morning Glories, 56–61, *57*, **58–61**
Multicolor knitting, 4, 14–15, *15*, 61

Needle felting, 75
Needle-Felted Hat, 72–75, *73*, **74–75**
Needles, 5–6, **6**

Picking up dropped stitches, 11, *11*
Pillbox Flowers, 44–47, *45*, **46–47**
Pompoms, 17, *17*
Psso (pass slip stitch over stitch), 8, 12, *12*

Running stitch for sewing seams, 16, *16*

Seams, sewing, 16, *16*
Sherpa Hat, Felted, 76–81, *77–78*, **78–79**, *80*, **81**
Sizing (fitting) hats, 8
Slip-a-Color, 32–35, *33*, **34–35**, *35*
Slipping a stitch purlwise, 34, *34*
Sport-weight yarn, 5
Ssk2tog (slip, slip, knit 2 stitches together), 8,
   12, *12*
Straight needles, 5
Stripes in the round, 14, *14*
Substituting yarn, 5

Tassels, 17, *17*
Telford, Barbara, 48, 56, 93
Tension (gauge), 7, *7*
Textured yarns, 65
Three-Gauge Beret, 40–43, *41, 42*
Three-In-One, 26–31, *27*, **28–31**
Twisted-knit cast on, *47*

UK/US size needles, **6**

Walker, Cynthia, 76, 81, 93
Watch Cap, 22–25, *23*, **24–25**
Worsted-weight yarn, 5
Wrapping and turning (W&T), 88, 89

Yarn, 4–5

**another Storey title you might enjoy:**

knit mittens!

15 Cool Patterns to Keep You Warm

ROBIN HANSEN

Hardcover
ISBN 1-58017-483-3
Full-color photographs and
illustrations throughout
128 pages
**Available wherever books are sold.**